DEVELOPMENT
OF
NATIONALISM IN INDIA

SURVEY OF MODERN INDIA SERIES

DEVELOPMENT OF NATIONALISM IN INDIA

Edited by

RAJ KUMAR

ANMOL PUBLICATIONS PVT. LTD.

NEW DELHI-110002 (INDIA)

ANMOL PUBLICATIONS PVT. LTD.
4374/4B, Ansari Road, Daryaganj
New Delhi-110 002

Development of Nationalism in India

First Edition 1999

ISBN 81-261-0234-9

PRINTED IN INDIA

Published by J. L. Kumar for Anmol Publications Pvt. Ltd., New Delhi-110 002 and Printed at Mehra Offset Press, Delhi.

Contents

Contents

Preface

There is vast literature on the history of Modern India. We have been mainly influenced by Stanley Lane-Poole, J. N. Sarkar; R. S. Tripathi, Beni Prasad, P. Saren, A.L. Srivastava and S.B.P. Nigam. These writers have left a great legacy in the form of documents translated, articles and books written. Dr. Sita Ram Sharma has supervised this compilation, Archana Chaturvedi, S.S. Abidi and many other friends have helped in various ways and we are grateful to them.

Readers must be thankful to Mr. J. L. Kumar whose brain child this work is and who has most expeditiously published it in present form.

—Raj Kumar

CHAPTER 1

The Early Nationalist Activity

I

It has been generally assumed that the Indian national movement underwent a basic mutation in 1905 and possibly a second one in 1919. Consequently, it is customary to divide it into three distinct stages or periods. There is much to favour this division. However, the basic continuities and changes involved in this periodisation are a matter of some controversy. It is the basic hypothesis of this chapter that there has existed a general tendency to overlook some of the basic continuities from the early nationalist era, to see discontinuities or changes where none existed, and to overemphasise or wrongly interpret the changes that did occur.

The basic elements of a movement are: political objectives, programme and ideology, strategy and methods and techniques of political struggle, social base, and class or social character. The extent and character of the continuity and change in the Indian national movement can be and have been traced under each of these heads, though no Chinese wall exists between them and they inevitably interpenetrate. The first aspect—the aspect of political objectives, programme, and ideology—is being left out of discussion except to point out briefly that the basic political objectives of the early nationalists were: to help the process of unifying Indian people into a nation, to introduce modern politics based on the doctrine of the sovereignty of the people and on the notion that politics is not the preserve of the ruling classes only, to create among the Indian people the feeling of self-confidence, to create an all India national political leadership or headquarters, to generate, form and crystallise an anti-imperialist ideology, to promote the growth of modern capitalist economy, and in the end to create a broad all India national movement. In the process, they also undertook an analysis of the basic character of British colonialism in India and to spread their understanding of its exploitative character among the Indian people. They created a national political platform and programme on which all Indians belonging to different regions, religions and social classes could agree and which could serve as the basis for all-India political activity, whose basic aim was not good government but democratic self-government. The later nationalists were in the main to build on their programme and their concrete exposure of the character of British rule. Without discussing the point further, I may also state that a difference in political aim or goal—between self-government as in the colonies and complete independence—has been wrongly used to define the basic political difference between the early nationalists or Moderates and the Extremists or the militant nationalists. After all, the Moderate nationalists were as much and as basically interested in the question of political power as the militant nationalists.[1] The exact verbalisation of the demand for Indian political power was a function of the emotional needs of the time, tactics, and relation of political forces. After all, Tilak and Gandhi had no hesitation in going back again and again from the demand for complete independence to dominion status or evenless.[2] This is not to deny that at any particular moment, as in 1905-08 or 1927-29, basic questions of strategy and tactics might be involved, but then historical analysis should concentrate on these substantive questions rather than on the husk of their verbal forms or emotional coating or symbols.

II

The overall strategy of the national movement was basically the same in all the three periods; only one of its aspects undergoing a basic change.

(A) Firstly, the Moderate nationalists laid down that the struggle for freedom was to be peaceful and bloodless. Political progress was to be harmonised with and based on order. This continued to be a basic tenet of the dominant leadership of the national movement up to the end. Only some of the Extremist leaders deviated from it in theory. But, in practice, they too operated within its basic framework. This tenet was to serve as a basic guarantee to the propertied classes that they would at no time be faced with a situation in which their interests might be put in jeopardy even temporarily.

(B) Secondly, the Moderates did not assign an important role to the masses or to mass struggle in their work. They assumed that for the time being political activity was to be confined to the stratum of the educated or to the "educated classes", as they put it. In part, behind this assumption lay the belief that political action by this narrow social stratum would suffice. But even more, they believed such a limitation to be objectively inevitable. Even when they saw in abstract the need for active participation by the masses, they lacked confidence in the capacity of the Indian masses to take part in modern politics for a long time to come. When they looked at the Indian masses they only saw their apathy and ignorance, their very real social, cultural and political backwardness, and not their energy, tenacity, and capacity to make sacrifices and to fight heroically.[3] Consequently, the task of politicalising and mobilising the masses was seen as an extremely slow one. They believed that militant mass struggles against imperialism could be waged only after the heterogeneous elements of Indian society had been welded into a nation and the inert masses fully politicalised, politically educated, and organised. In its turn the absence of a mass base led them to political moderation. Lacking mass support, they walked charily, confined their political work to agitation and propaganda, and felt that the time was not ripe for throwing a challenge to the powerful foreign rulers. To do so would be to invite premature repression and destruction of the existing political movement.[4] It may be noted that the Moderates were not very wrong in seeing the immensity of the task involved in politicalising, mobilising, and activising the politically inert masses. But instead of undertaking the task, they tended to be overwhelmed by the prospects of doing so.

The most important, and perhaps the only significant, shift in the nationalist political strategy came on this point. Tilak, Bipin Chandra Pal, and other Extremist leaders had infinite faith in the power of the masses in action and in the Indian people's capacity to bear the strain of a prolonged political struggle against imperialism. They believed that suppression by the government would not throttle the mass movement. It would, instead, educate the people, arouse them further, strengthen their resolve to overthrow imperialism, and lead to a heightened political struggle. They therefore advocated the organisation of a mass struggle against imperialism and as a first step the taking of politics to the masses.[5] They talked of bridging the gulf between the educated and the masses. Some of them did reach out to the masses, for example, Ashwini Kumar Dutt in Barisal.

But while recognising this break from the Moderate era, we may also make a distinction between the hope and the fulfilment. For one, even at the height of the Extremist movement in Bengal, the peasantry was not mobilised. The alienation between the educated Extremist political workers and the masses was not lessened to any significant extent. In fact, the Extremists did not even know how to go about the task. In practice what they succeeded in doing was to spread the movement deeper among the lower middle classes who were already brought within the ambit of nationalism in the Moderate era. Tilak and others did talk of the people but their people turned out to be the educated and half-educated segments of the urban and semi-urban petty bourgeoisie and, most of all, the educated youth among them. It is therefore not correct to say that Tilak 'identified himself with the masses' or that he brought 'the masses of the people's into politics. Tilak himself accepted in 1907 that he was the leader primarily of the educated Indians.[6] Lajpat Rai too frankly acknowledged in 1908 that the political movement in India had to depend on the educated because of the backwardness and apathy of the masses.[7]

Similarly, the Extremists failed to evolve an adequate technique of political 'action'. Despite their sharp criticism of the Moderates for confining the movement to mere agitation, their own practice could not basically transcend agitation, though their agitation was much more militant and effective. They undoubtedly evolved a higher concept of the forms of struggle,[8] but they were unable to implement this higher concept. They remained at the ideological-critical level. This failure of the Extremists inevitably led to revolutionary terrorism. Since most of the Extremist leaders had wrongly defined their differences with the Moderates—they had concentrated on 'action' and sacrifice rather than on the need to evolve a different type of politics—the young men brought up on the ideology of 'action' and sacrifice were soon disenchanted with militant agitation, demanded 'action', and took recourse to individual terrorism. Ironically, the political struggle or 'action' of these heroic youth also turned out to be, so far as it had political impact, a form of agitation, or as they themselves defined it, "propaganda by deed".

Gandhi too had an immense faith in the Indian people.[9] He based his entire politics on their militancy and self-sacrificing spirit. He made the sharpest break with the Moderate tradition by reaching down to the masses, arousing them to political activity, and bringing them into the forefront of the struggle. This was the revolutionary aspect of the Gandhian period of the nationalist struggle. Moreover, Gandhi alone discovered a new and viable method of political struggle and mass action, thus enabling him to immediately capture the leadership of the movement and to retain it till the end. But even in these respects, four serious limitations need to be carefully noted: (i) The extent to which the Gandhian movement politicalised and involved the masses has not yet been carefully researched and is often exaggerated. I may hazard the opinion that the agricultural labourers and poor peasants in most parts of the country and the masses in general in several parts were not brought into the political process or even touched by nationalist politics, so that the social base of the national movement was still not very strong in 1947.

(ii) While the masses were moved into action they were never politically organised in spite of the four-anna membership. They remained outside the Congress organisational structure—always waiting in the wings to act.

(iii) The gulf between the intelligentsia, which still provided the leadership of the movement, and the masses still lay largely unbridged in spite of some aspects of Gandhian mass work. Even the left wing was to fail in the task.

(iv) Above all, the political activity of the masses was rigidly controlled from the top. The masses never became an independent political force. The question of their participation in the decision-making process was never even raised. The masses were always to remain—to coin a phrase—'passive actors' or 'extras' whose political activity remained under the rigid control of middle class leaders and within the confines of the needs of bourgeois social development. Herein also lay the crucial role of the way non-violence was defined and practised by Gandhi. I may also point out here that the crucial weakness of the Gandhian movement and its essential continuity with the earlier tradition of keeping the movement within the bourgeois framework did not lie in the refusal to take recourse to militant forms of struggle or in the predominance of non-violent forms, as left-wing critics from M. N. Roy onwards have so often maintained. The question of the forms of struggle is after all an aspect of time and space, of the concrete historical situation. This weakness lay in the utterly restricted and subordinated role of the masses in the political struggle, in the complete absence of any mechanism or channel through which they could influence the course of the struggle or its outcome. This question did not arise in the first phase of the movement because political activity was manifestly confined to the intelligentsia. But later, when the masses were mobilised for the movement, the pattern of leadership and control remained the same as before 1905.[10]

(C) Thirdly, crucial to the Moderate strategy of political advance was another feature which also became the basic feature of the later nationalist strategy, thus establishing a basic continuity in all the three phases of the movement. The Moderates assumed that political rights and self-government should grow slowly but steadily, 'from precedent to precedent', and by progressive stages. Thus the process of national liberation was not to be that of a prolonged revolution but that of a prolonged stage-by-stage evolution. The growth was moreover to occur through the tactics of pressure—negotiations, compromise, and concessions—pressure P-C-P and not through the seizure of power or expulsion of the foreign rulers. Four basic assumptions were involved in this strategy: (i) The function of political work and agitation, whether in India or Britain, was to put pressure on the colonial authorities to concede the immediate demands. (ii) Given enough pressure, the authorities could be persuaded to give concessions. This was a crucial assumption. The British must cooperate in the process *since the changes were to be brought through their actions.* (iii) Every concession must be utilised and worked. This would necessarily involve cooperating with the colonial regime 'as best as they could'. (iv) Every compromise must be seen as a jumping ground for the next one and, therefore, agitation or pressure should be quickly renewed. This spiralling movement would continue till the goal of Indian political power was reached. This entire strategy was summarised with great clarity and brilliance by gopal Krishna Gokhale in 1907:

> Constitutional agitation was agitation by methods which they were entitled to adopt to bring about the changes they desired through the action of constituted authorities. . . . *The changes desired must be obtained only through the action of constituted authorities by bringing to bear on them the pressure of public opinion* . . . . Three things were excluded—rebellion, aiding or abetting a foreign invasion, and resort to crime. Roughly speaking, barring these three things, all else was constitutional . . . . As regards the second condition, namely, that *redress must be obtained through the constituted authorities, it was clear that implied constant pressure being brought to bear on the authorities,* and the idea that they should have nothing to do with the authorities was not one to be entertained. *The pressure exerted undoubtedly depended upon the strength and determination of the public opinion behind it,* and the necessity of building up that strength and hardening that determination was obviously paramount. But the idea that they should leave the authorities severely alone *and seek to attain their goal independently of them was inadmissible and absured.*[11]

Similarly, in his Presidential Address to the National Congress of 1905, he had said:

> The goal of the Congress is that India should be governed in the interests of the Indians themselves, and that, *in course of time,* a form of government should be attained in this country similar to what exists in the Self-Governing colonies of the British Empire . . . . That advance, moreover, can only be gradual, as at each stage of the progress it may be necessary for us to pass through a brief course of apprenticeship before we are enabled to go to the next one.[12]

The Moderates assumed that the force of the public opinion of the educated Indians and of the British democratic opinion would suffice to provide the pressure that was to set the entire mechanism in operation. These assumptions were ridiculed by the later nationalists as in fact also by the contemporary colonial administrators and statesmen. It should, however, be clearly seen that what changed after 1905 was the nature of the political pressure that was to be brought to bear upon the rulers and not the basic strategy of pressure-compromise-pressure leading to political advance that could be brought about through the actions of 'the duly constituted authorities'. Tilak and Gandhi too were not working for the direct overthrow of British rule. They too emphasised 'the technique of negotiations backed by controlled mass action'. The aim of every one of their movements was to compel the British to negotiate and give concessions; and nearly every one of these movements ended with concessions and negotiations, overt or covert, direct or by proxy.

Because the later nationalists gave several calls for immediate independence, it is easy to be misled into thinking that their strategic approach was different. In fact, such calls were a part of the same main design. It is, for example, interesting that after every such call, Gandhi came out with a set of immediate demands, e.g., the famous eleven demands of 1930, which had little direct relation to the demand for immediate and complete independence made by the Lahore Congress a few days earlier.

The later nationalists did of course change—and this was historically very significant—the mode of persuasion or putting pressure. They put greater and mass pressure behind their demands. They shifted from intellectuals to the masses, from memorials, petitions, and resolutions to processions, demonstrations and vast mass movements. The sanctions behind their demands were different and far stronger. But the political advance was still to occur by stages and through compromise, that is, ultimately through British consent and action.[13]

The very forms of struggle adopted were suited only to this strategic design. The Gandhian mass movement contained no mechanism for the seizure of power. In this respect the question of violence or non-violence was a red herring in the path, whether thrown by the right or the left. The fact was that the Gandhian forms of struggle could only exert pressure on the authorities up to a point. They could not lead to positive revolutionary action such as the peaceful occupation of schools and colleges (in place of their boycott), police thanas, *Kutcheries* (courts) (creation of alternative courts of justice rather than their mere boycott), and other government offices, and even foreign firms, banks, and factories, or the peaceful disarming of the army.[14] They could not and did not create alternative organs of social management or power or even elementary appurtenances of an alternative regime which, and not violence, are the essence of a revolution. Even a non-violent movement could have posed a challenge to the sovereignty of the foreigner and become the starting point of the seizure of power remaining non-violent in the beginning, jut as a phase of violence could be used as pressure in the P-C-P strategy. But the very essence of the Gandhian strategy was to compel the enemy to negotiate and concede demands. This is the major reason why an important aspect of the Gandhian programme, the non-payment of taxes, which *would* pose a challenge to the sovereignty of the state was *never* put into practice on a significant scale. It could have put massive pressure on the government to come to the negotiating table and offer concessions, but it could also have escalated into a total confrontation.

Therefore, the crucial significance in Gandhian political philosophy of the notion of bringing about a change in the enemy's heart, of keeping the door open to negotiations, of the very definition of non-violence as not wanting to hurt the enemy in thought, word, or deed, but of converting him, and of the sharp distinction between civil disobedience and 'civil licence'. Hence, after having initiated a movement, Gandhi could but wait either to be arrested or to be called to the negotiating table. The former produced a temporary deadlock that was soon broken by a new round of negotiations conducted directly or through intermediaries. In either case, the result was new political concessions. Sometimes the concessions were the result of negotiations and an officially arrived at compromise. At other times, no negotiations took place on surface. But concessions, in such cases often highly unsatisfactory ones, came all the same. Gandhi would then cut the losses and quietly agree to work the resulting reforms. He would not sign an agreement since that would be highly demoralising and even unmanly, but, while keeping himself aloof, he would sanction participation in the official political process by his co-leaders as he did in 1924 and 1935-36, or even in 1947 when, though unhappy with the manner of the transfer of power, he used his personal prestige to persuade the All India Congress Committee to accept the negotiated compromise. In fact, this strategy of pressure and compromise can be studied in all its complexity and intricacy in the pre-1942 and the post-1945 political activities and tactics of Gandhi and other Congress leaders.

III

The changing social base of the national movement was one of the elements of change in its three phases. In the early Moderate phase it was extremely narrow, being limited to the urban educated Indians. Having noted this, it must be pointed out that even in this phase the movements continuously widened its social base to include fresh social strata, especially sections of the lower middle classes. This is clearly revealed by the steady growth and spread of vernacular newspapers. Nor was this growth fortuitous. Most of the early nationalist leaders, for example, Dadabhai Naoroji, Surendranath Banerjee, K.T.Telang, Ranade, V.V. Agarkar, Tilak, Gokhale, G. Subramaniya Iyer, K.K. Mitra, Ganga Prasad Varma, Madan Mohan Malaviya, and Rampal Singh, were connected with Indian language newspapers.

It is at the same time important to remember that this social base did not, as is often assumed, include the industrial and commercial bourgeoisie or the zamindars and landlords. In fact, it was with the help of the landed magnates, the urban rich merchants and capitalists, and the elderly old-style politicians that the British officials hoped during the 1880s to counteract the 'radical', 'extremist', and 'disloyal and seditionist' political elements represented by the Congress. The upper class Indians—the merchants, industrialists, zamindars, as also the successful lawyers, doctors, and civil servants—did not yet give any meaningful financial support to the movement[15] with the result that most of the early political workers had to earn their own livelihood[16] and their political organisations such as the National Congress were virtually starved of funds, functioned on shoe-string budgets, and were consequently severely inhibited in their political work. There was a reverse side to this phenomenon. Political activity without the massive financial support of the rich was possible precisely because of its modest scale. Vast mass movements, large scale election campaigns, wide-ranging agitations, and large political machineries based on an army of cadres, which were the dominant feature of the Gandhian era from 1919 to 1947, could not be organised without equally large financial resources. This made the movement dependent on the generosity of the rich. The early nationalists escaped this dependence on the bourgeoisie by the very character of their political activity!

As is well known, the social base of the Extremists lay primarily in the urban lower middle classes whom they succeeded in politicalising in some parts of the country. Interestingly, the capitalists withheld their support from the Extremists in spite of their vigorous campaign of Swadeshi and Boycott. Later, during the days of the Home Rule Leagues, only a few stray capitalists gave financial help to the two Leagues. Also, while the Extremists talked glowingly of the masses in general, they too like the Moderates tended to revert to a middle class self-consciousness whenever faced with the masses in flesh and blood—the peasantry or the working class.

The masses—the peasants and workers—came into the national movement primarily in the Gandhian era. This is perhaps the most important aspect of the growth of the national movement. But it is no less important—and this is often ignored—that the capitalists as a class also came into the movement, and came to support it actively, though primarily financially, only during this era. Neither the Moderates nor the Extremists had been able to get the active support of this class since both the class and its contradiction with imperialism matured fully only during and after the First World War. Moreover, the Moderate and Extremist movements were not socially or politically significant enough for the capitalist class to make a determined attempt to dominate them. But once the national movement became a powerful mass movement, the bourgeoisie could not afford to have it turn against itself by continuing to pursue the earlier policy of apathy and neglect towards it. Thus, to repeat, the extension of the social base of the movement to the capitalist class was as important and new a feature of the movement in its Gandhian phase as its extension to the workers and peasants.

Another aspect of the mass character of the movement and the militant character of its nationalism after 1918 was the general sucking in for the first time, except for a short period in Bengal from 1905-1907, of the large strata of small zamindars and landlords and merchants and money-lenders. It was also only now that the urban and semi-urban lower middle classes were fully drawn into the movement on a national scale.

Moreover, despite its activity encompassing different social classes and strata, its basic thrust throughout its three stages came primarily from the activity and commitment of the petty bourgeoisie or the motley and diverse social strata often covered by the blanket term 'the middle classes'. The petty bourgeoisie was the chief source of the movement's cadre and activists as also of its psychology and ethos.

IV

Assertions of changes in the class or social character of the Indian national movement have come from two different quarters. One school of nationalist writers asserts that the early nationalists represented the upper classes or at the most the educated elite, that the Extremists represented either the people or at least the lower, non-upper class segments of society, and that Gandhi represented the hungry, naked and oppressed peasant thus making the national movement a people's movement. The other school, consisting of many Marxist and semi-Marxist writers, suggests that the early nationalists represented the upper or big bourgeoisie or the big commercial bourgeoisie which was often collaborationist that the Extremists represented the petty bourgeoisie and that under Gandhi the national movement became a full-scale bourgeois movement, representing the overall interests of the bourgeoisie in general and the industrial capitalist class in particular.

In my opinion both these schools are wrong in their class characterisation of the different phases of the national movement. In fact, we have here another basic, perhaps the most important, continuity, for the class character of the national movement was the same throughout from its inception to 1947. It was a bourgeois democratic movement, this is, it represented the interests of all classes and segments of Indian society vis-a-vis imperialism but under the hegemony of the industrial bourgeoisie. In this respect, Tilak and Gandhi were no different from the Moderates; they were no less bourgeois.

Involved in this discussion are both the historiographic principles that enable one to determine the class character of a movement or to answer the questions whom does the movement represent and how does it do so and the application of these principles so the reality of the Indian national movement. Historians of different hues have in general used three distinct criteria to determine and establish the class or social character of a movement.

(1) Social base of the movement or the participation in it of diffeerent social strata and classes.

(2) Class or social origins and characteristics of the men and women who exercise the actual leadership function and who may, therefore, be described as its leaders in the narrow, functional sense.

(3) The character of its political and economic programme, policies and ideology.

I would suggest (i) that the first two criteria are historiographically or sociologically the wrong way to go about the task; (ii) that even their application does not prove the two commonly found assertions regarding the social or class character of the Indian national movement during its different phases; and (iii) that the application of the third, correct criterion does not show any significant change or discontinuity in this character.

(A) The social base of a movement does introduce many types of constraints on a movement and is, therefore, in itself one of its significant aspects, but it cannot determine its class content. Another way of saying the same thing is that the nature of social participation in a movement and its class content or social character are two different aspects. A movement does not necessarily represent the interests of the majority of its participants any more than an army fights for the interests of its soldiers or a party for those of its voters.

A movement can bear the same class character whether its social base is narrow or wide. Similarly, the extent of mass action and the militancy of the forms of struggle are also not the decisive determinants in this regard. These are matters of historical conjuncture. The capitalists too may want struggle, promote it, or at least tolerate it under specific historical conditions. In history the bourgeoisie has often aroused the masses, brought them into motion and even promoted armed struggle. The real question is not that of the social base or the forms of political struggle but of the social hegemony over the movement. Thus in India the bourgeoisie did not see a mass movement as a threat to its interests so long as it was confined within limits that did not threaten its hegemony over social development. And here it may be suggested that while the Moderates established bourgeois ideological hegemony over the small social segment of the intelligentsia, the political leadership of the Gandhian era established bourgeois ideological political and organisational hegemony over the vast mass of peasants, workers, and lower middle classes.[17] Thus, even though the mass bases of the Moderates, Extremists and Gandhi were so very different, the movements led by them were equally bourgeois nationalist in character.

Lastly, if the social base of a movement determined its social character, the Moderate and the Extremist phases could not be described as bourgeois at all, since we have already seen that the capitalists and their money came into the movement effectively only after 1918!

(B) It can also be asserted as general principle that though the social origins of a leadership have undoubtedly powerful though indirect effects on the programme, policies, ideology, and forms of action of a movement, they do not determine its social character. Witness, for example, the social origins of the founders and leaders of the socialist movement in the modern era. What is of equal significance in the present case is the fact that the social origins and modes of existence of the national leadership were virtually the same throughout the three stages. The national leadership from 1880 to 1947 can be best characterised as nationalist intelligentsia. The direct leadership of the movement was never in the hands of the capitalists or the masses or even the lower middle classes, but was monopolised by the middle class nationalist intellectuals. This was frankly recognised by the Moderates, Tilak, Gandhi, Nehru and others. Thus, the lawyers, doctors, journalists, and the self-maintained whole-time political workers of middle class origin continued to dominate the leadership from the beginning to the end.

It is generally recognised that during the Extremist and the Gandhian periods the leaders represented social groups other than those to which they themselves belonged. But the earlier nationalist leaders are often supposed to constitute a class in itself, namely, the class of educated Indians. But in fact as a 'class' they were so few in numbers at the time that they could have been readily accommodated within the colonial structure, as Ripon and others desired. Dufferin made a serious attempt to do so by advocating the active association of the educated Indians with the administration and 'the conduct of affairs of their country' by widening the membership of the legislative councils as well as the scope for their employment in the public services. He would placate the early political workers so long as they behaved as a narrow class, but not when they put forward demands which transcended their own class demands when they claimed to be the spokesman of the people against foreign rule, when their political programme and activities could not be accommodated within the colonial structure. The Montford

Report was still to advocate 30 years later a similar policy towards the nationalists as spokesman of the educated Indians. In fact, the continuous tradition of liberal-labour regret at the failure of the conservative British ruling elite to settle with the Moderates by giving them a role to play in British India has been based on this false premise. But since the Moderates' basic terms were anti-imperialist, such an accommodation was not possible except as temporary truce. Dufferin and other conservatives had the insight to see this. They rightly viewed the early nationalists not as a 'class' but as the advance-guard intellectuals of nationalism whose political activity would invariably lead to confrontation with the authorities and to anti-imperialism. The early nationalists can, therefore, be best characterised as nationalist intellectuals who were bourgeois in their thought and life style. They were anti-imperialist from a bourgeois point of view rather than any so-called middle-class point of view.

(C) In their programme and ideology, the early nationalists worked for the creation of a modern bourgeois state, economy and society in the image of the most advanced bourgeois state, economy and society of the day. Their programme represented the interests of all classes in so far as they came into conflict with imperialism. At the same time, they kept out all issues and demands which would bring one section of the Indian society into conflict with another. There was little in their programme to arouse the uneducated peasants, workers, or the urban poor. Their entire programme was bourgeois in so far as it was confined within the broad parameters of bourgeois social development. As intellectuals, they militantly propagated the cause of the industrial bourgeoisie even though it failed to give them its support.

Once the issue is posed in this way, it becomes obvious that the national leadership of the Extremist and Gandhian era also represented a similar bourgeois social order. Neither Tilak nor Gandhi transcended the Moderate economic and political programme or social vision. Tilak or the Bengal Extremits did not make any advance over the Moderates so far as advocacy of the interests of the masses was concerned. Nor did Gandhi in this respect go beyond the Moderates in thought, word, or deed, at least till the 1940s. In spite of his 'passionate sense of identity with the lowly and the oppressed'. He did not take up in any of his major political campaigns and movements the peasant demands for the reduction of rent, lessening of the debt burden, and protection from oppression by the police and other lower officials, not to speak of land redistribution. For example, in the famous Eleven Demands presented to the government in 1930 as representing the minimum national terms for a settlement and constituting, in his own words, "the substance of independence", Gandhi included the capitalist demands for the restoration of the exchange rate to 1s. 4d., a protective tariff against foreign cloth, and the reservation of coastal trade for Indian shipping. But the only peasant demand to be included was for the reduction of land revenue. This last demand was one of the main items of agitation in the Moderate armoury also.

Thus Gandhi and Tilak were as much the ideological and political representatives of the industrial bourgeoisie as the Moderates in the sense that they viewed national interest from the point of view of the industrial bourgeoisie, and that once they had broken the hold of imperialist ideological hegemony over the minds of the Indian people, they all helped structure bourgeois hegemony over Indian civil society. They led and educated the people to accept that the bourgeois path of social development was the only available alternative to colonial development. It may, however, be noted that while the Moderates and the Extremists made this choice when no other model of social development was available to the Indian people and intelligentsia in theory, or reality the Gandhian era nationalists did so when the socialists alternative was not only readily available both in ideology and real life but was in fact a keen competitor nationally and internationally. Moreover, the hegemony of the bourgeoisie over the national movement was, if anything even more firmly clamped down in the Gandhian era than before. On the other hand, one may venture to suggest that subjectively Dadabhai Naoroji, Surendranath Banerjee, or Gopal Krishna Gokhale were no less inspired by noble ideals and the love of the people than Tilak or Gandhi.

NOTES

1. Tilak repeatedly pointed out that there were no real differences between him and the Moderates on the goals of the national movement. Thus, in 1907 at the height of the political struggle with the Moderates, he said in his important speech on "The Tenets of the New Party": ". . . the government of one country by another can never be a successful, and therefore a permanent government. There is no difference of opinion about this fundamental proposition between the Old and New Schools." *Bal Gangadhar Tilak, His Writings and Speeches,* enlarged edition, 1919, p. 56.

2. Tilak told H. W. Nevinson in 1907: "Certainly there is a very small party which talks about abolishing the British rule at once and completely. That does not concern us: it is much too far in the future. Unorganised disarmed, and still disunited, we should not have a chance of shaking the British suzerainty. We may leave all that sort of thing to a distant time." Quoted in H. W. Nevinson, *New Spirit in India,* 1908, p. 72. For 1916, see his famous Home Rule Speech at Belgium, *op. cit.,* pp. 108-18. Gandhi went back to Dominion Status after having given a call for *Purna Swaraj* in 1920-22. Similarly, he was willing to negotiate for far less during 1931, even though the Civil Disobedience Movement had been launched in 1930 around the Complete Independence Resolution of the 1929 Congress Session.

3. Describing the difficulties in the way of the organisation of active political struggle, Gokhale referred in 1907 to "The vast masses of the people of the country lying inert and apathetic, . . . deplorably divided and aub-divided . . . plunged in abject poverty and ignorance, and wedded to usages and institutions which . . . were not exactly calculated to promote vigorous, sustained or combined action for purposes of progress." *Speeches,* second ed., Natesan & Co. edition, n.d., p. 1103.

4. At the Surat Congress in 1907, Gokhale told the militants: "You do not realise the enormous reserve of power behind the government. If the Congress were to do anything such as you suggest, the government would have no difficulty in throttling it in 5 minutes." Quoted in Andres and Mukherji, *The Rise and Growth of the Congress in India,* 1938, p. 215.

5. Thus, Bipin Chandra Pal said in his famous Madras lectures in 1907: "There is anther attitude that—with the decadence of the faith in the foreign people and in the foreign government, with the decadence of our faith in the foreign administration which

has come to us, we have learnt to look nearer home. Our eyes have been turned away from the Government House, away from the Houses of Parliament, from Simla and Calcutta, and our faces have turned now to the starving, the naked, the patient and long-suffering 300 millions of our people, and in it we see a new potency, because we view them now with an eye of love which we never had felt before, and in the teeming, toiling, starving and naked populations of India, we find *possibilities, potentialities, germs that have given rise to this New Movement. That is the corner-stone of this Movement, namely, Faith in the People, Faith in the genius of the Nation.* Faith in God, who has been guiding the genius of this nation through ages by historic evolution, Faith in the eternal destiny of the Indian people. With the decadence of our faith in the foreign government and in the foreign nation, has grown up this higher, this dearer, this deeper, this more vital and more divine faith in Indian humanity (cheers). And to understand the New Movement properly, you must look upon it through the prism of this new faith in the Indian people." *Swadeshi and Swaraj,* 1954, pp. 137-38. Emphasis added.

6. Tilak, *op. cit.*, pp. 69-73, 374 and 382.

7. Lajpat Rai, *Young India,* Indian edition, pp. 91-92.

8. See Tilak, op. cit., p. 65; Bipin Chandra Pal, op. cit., pp. 216-20, and 241-49: Lajpat Rai, op. cit., p. 141; Aurobindo Ghosh, *Doctrine of Passive Resistance,* 1948.

9. Referring to the common people, who had participated in the South African struggle, in the course of his reply to an address of welcome in Madras in 1915, he said: "You have said that I inspired those great men and whom, but I cannot accept that proposition. It was they, the simple-minded folk, who worked away in faith, never expecting the slightest reward, who inspired me, who kept me to the proper level, and who compelled me by their great sacrifice, by their great faith, by their great trust in the great God to do the work that I was able to do." *Collected Works,* Vol. XIII, 1964, pp. 52-53.

10. Already by the end of the nineteenth century some leaders were complaining that all real decision making powers were being exercised by the established leadership at the top with the rank and file being left in the cold. This was to become a perpetual complaint of the Congress rank and file in the later years.

11. Gokhale, op. cit., pp. 1105-06. Emphasis added. Justice Ranade had explained one aspect of this strategy as follows: "Moderation

implies the conditions of never vainly aspiring after the impossible or after too remote ideals, but striving each day to take the next step in the order of natural growth that lies nearest to our hands in a spirit of compromise and fairness." Quoted in T. V. Paravate, *Gopal Krishna Gokhale,* 1959, p. 463.

12. Gokhale, op. cit., pp. 829-30. Emphasis added. It is to be noted that going to the next stage is as important as passing through a brief course of apprenticeship or a halt at each stage.

13. The following extracts from one of Tilak's speeches in 1907 are quite revealing in this respect: " . . . the Proclamation (of 1858) remained a dead letter, because you could not get it enforced .... A promise was made but you proved too weak to have it enforced . . . . Is Mr. Morley going to fulfil it? The explanation of the Proclamation is not the question. The question is what will compel him to fulfil it. (Nationalists must compel but it is he who will fulfil. B.C.) . . . I admit that we must ask; but we must ask with the consciousness that the demand cannot be refused . . . . We say prepare your forces, organise your power, and then go to work *so that they cannot refuse you what you demand* . . . . I want the whole bread and that immediately. But if I cannot get the whole, don't think that I have no patience. I will *take the half they give me and then try for the remainder.*" Op. cit., pp. 62, 64, 66. Also see p. 45. Emphasis added. H. W. Nevinson reported Tilak as having told him in 1907: "The immediate question for us is how we are to bring pressure on bureaucracy . . . . It is only in our answer to that question that we differ from the so-called Moderates. They still hope to influence public opinion in England by sending deputations (etc.) . . . We Extremists have determined on other methods." Quoted in Nevinson, op. cit., pp. 73-74. Similarly Gandhi summed up his basic political approach in the following advice he gave to the leaders of the states' people's struggles in 1939: "I am convinced that direct negotiations should be opened with the authorities. Hitherto, the State Congress people have talked at the authorities and the latter at them. The result has been a widening of the gulf between them. It would not do for a satyagrahi to argue that the approach must be mutual . . . . The first and the last work of a satyagrahi is ever to seek an opportunity for an honourable approach . . . If the leader have active ahimsa in them, they must cultivate a belief in the perfect possibility and necessity of such approach. And if they have that belief, the way will surely be open to them. In my own person, it is well known, I have always acted on that principle . . . . Our aim must remain what it is, but we must be prepared to negotiate

for less than the whole, so long as it is unmistakably of the same kind and has in it inherent possibility of expansion." *Collected Works,* Vol. LXIX, 1977, p. 323.

14. Interestingly, this is precisely what the peaceful crowds sometimes did spontaneously during the non-cooperation movements. In 1930, the people of Sholapur virtually replaced the police and organised volunteers to maintain order and to even regulate the traffic in the streets till the police provoked a clash. Punjab-style martial law and mass butchery were needed to control the situation. The case of the Garhwali soldiers refusing to fire on a Pathan crowd and handing over their rifles, all very peacefully, is quite well known.

15. The generosity of J. N. Tata to the National Congress is nothing but a canard. He contributed to the Congress only 1000 rupees spread over two years and that too in the heat of anger against the imposition of cotton excise duties in 1896. It was only a few patriotic zamindars and princes who contributed in a significant manner to the nationalist causes; but they did so entirely in their personal capacity and not as spokesmen or even members of their class.

16. This lack of funds partially explains the predominance of lawyers and journalists—the two independent professionals—among the early nationalist leaders. They were independent in a dual sense: they were independent of government control and they were not dependent upon rich men's contributions for their capacity to carry on in politics. On the other hand, Gokhale and Surendranath Banerjee had to divert a large part of their time to teaching undergraduates. Tilak had to run coaching classes for the law students for several years till his newspapers came out of the red. G. Subramaniya Iyer and Bipin Chandra Pal were working journalists.

17. It has been often asserted regarding Gandhi that the peasantry 'always stood at the centre of his thought and action'. I do not agree. He did not take up any of its major demands against the zamindars, landlords, merchants, and money-lenders. At the centre of his thought stood national freedom which would broadly remain confined within a bourgeois framework of social development. He undoubtedly had great sympathy for the peasants and understood their urges and psychology. He used this understanding to draw them into the national struggle. But to have this understanding and to use the psychology of a class to activise it is very different from saying that this class 'stood at

the centre of his thought and action'. For example, Hitler, a direct 'opposite' of Gandhi, too had a brilliant and deep understanding of the psychology of the German petty bourgeoisie and he used it effectively to capture power by organising a popular movement. The difference between Hitler and Gandhi was that the former harnessed petty bourgeois psychology to the historically regressive task of maintaining monopoly capitalism and establishing the barbaric fascist political system, which Gandhi used peasant psychology for the progressive task of overthrowing imperialism and contributing to the establishment of a bourgeois democratic state.

CHAPTER 2

Three Stages of National Struggle

"I am sorry to say that if no instruction had been addressed in political crises to the people of this country except to remember to hate violence, to love order and to exercise patience, the liberties of this country would never have been obtained."
—William Ewart Gladstone.

The development of Indian Nationalism over half a century would require a separate study for any adequate treatment, since it comprises the entire political history of a people passing through the most critical stages of their struggle for national unity and freedom. For the immediate purposes, however, of throwing light on the present political situation what is most important is to see sharply the outstanding landmarks of that development and the main successive tendencies which have played their parts and helped to build up the character of the present movement.

The historical development of Indian Nationalism is marked by three great waves of struggle, each at a successively higher level, and early leaving its permanent marks on the movement and opening the way to a new phase. In its earliest phase Indian Nationalism, as we have seen, reflected only the big bourgeoisie— the progressive elements among the land-owners the new industrial bourgeoisie and the well-to-do intellectual elements. The first great wave of unrest which disturbed these placid waters, in the period preceding 1914, reflected the discontent of the urban petty bourgeoisie but did not yet reach the masses. The role of the masses in the national movement, alike of the peasantry and of the new force of the industrial working class emerged only after the war of 1914-18. Two great waves of mass struggle developed, the first in the years immediately succeeding the war, the second in the years succeeding the world economic crisis. On the basis of this record of struggle. Indian Nationalism stands today at its highest point of strength since its inception. The National Congress following its sweeping election victory of 1946 and its control of the Ministries in the majority of the provinces, has reached a decisive representative position, and now faces the most critical responsibilities of leadership. Once again today the national movement stands at the parting of the ways. It is evident to all observers that a great new period of struggle, which may prove decisive for the fate of British rule in India and for the future of the Indian people, is now opening. In relation to the problems of this present situation a rapid survey may be taken of these previous stages of struggle and their lessons.

1. The First Great Wave of Struggle (1905-1910)

For twenty years the National Congress developed along the path laid down by its founders. During these twenty years no basic claim for self-government in any form—that is, no basic national claim—was formulated in its resolution but only the demand for a greater degree of Indian representation within the British system of rule. The maximum demand was for representative institutions, not yet for self-government. The outlook of the early moderate leaders may be found expressed in the statement of one of the ablest— and most moderate—of their number, Romesh Chandra Dutt, President of the Congress in 1890, who formulated the demand of "the people of India" in the following terms in 1901:

> "The people of India are not fond of sudden changes and revolutions. They do not ask for new constitutions, issuing like armed Minervas from the heads of legislative Jupiters. They prefer to work on lines which have already been laid down. They desire to strengthen the present government, and to bring it more in touch with the people. They desire to see some Indian members in the Secretary of State's Council and in the Viceroy's Executive Council, representing

> Indian agriculture and industries. They wish to see Indian members in an Executive Council for each Province. They wish to represent the interests of the Indian people in the discussion of every important administrative of question. They seek that the administration the Empire and its great provinces should be conducted with the cooperation of the people.
>
> "There is a Legislative Council in each large Indian Province, and some of the members of these Councils are elected under the Act of 1892. The experiment has proved a success, and some expansion of these Legislative Councils would strengthen administration and bring it more in touch with the people . . . A Province with thirty districts and a population of thirty millions may fairly have thirty elected members on its Legislative Council. Each District should feel that it has some voice in the administration of the Province."
>
> (Romesh Chandra Dutt, 1901, Preface to "The Economic History of India" Vol. 1. "India Under Early British Rule," p. xviii).

The moderation of these demands correctly reflected the position of the early Indian bourgeoisie. The Congress of those days was exclusively representative of the upper bourgeoisie, and especially of its ideological representatives, the educated middle class. While it won an enthusiastic and wide response from these circles from the outset, so much so that measures had to be taken from an early date to restrict the number of delegates, that response was entirely confined to these social elements. "The four thousand gentlemen sitting round me", wrote an English Member of Parliament, W.S. Caine, who attended the 1889 Congress, "are picked men of the legal, medical, engineering and literary professions all over India." The early moderate leaders were well aware that they did not represent the masses, and that, while they might endeavour to speak as interpreters in the name of the people, they could not claim to speak as its voice. "The Congress," declared Sir Pherozeshah Mehta, the principal guiding leader of the Congress in its earlier years, "was indeed not the voice of the masses, but it was the duty of their educated compatriots to interpret their grievances and offer suggestions for their redress."

The early Indian bourgeoisie of that time understood very well that they were in no position to challenge British rule. On the contrary, they look to British rule as their ally. For them the main enemy was not British rule as such, but the backwardness of the people, the lack of modern development of the country, the strength of the forces of obscurantism and ignorance, and the administrative shortcomings of the "bureaucratic" system responsible for the situation. In their fight against these evil they looked hopefully for the co-operation of the British rulers. "The educated classes", declared Ananda Mohan Bose, President of the 1898 Congress, "are the friends and not the foes of England—her natural and necessary allies in the great work that lies before her." I have no fears", affirmed Sir Pherozeshah Mehta in 1890, "but that British statesmen will ultimately respond to the Call." Dadabai Naoroji, the Father of the Congress, when presiding over the Second Congress, appealed to the British rulers "not to drive this force (the educated Indians) into opposition instead of drawing it to your side." Surendra Nath Banerjee, the "silvertongued orator" of the older Congress leaders, proclaimed the ideal to "work with unwavering loyalty to the British connection—for the object was not the suppression of British rule in India, but the broadening of its basis, the liberalising of its spirit, the ennobling of its character and placing it on the unchangeable foundation of a nation's affections".[1]

It should not be assumed from the tone of these declarations that these early Congress leaders were reactionary antinational servants of alien rule. On the contrary, they represented at that time the most progressive force in Indian society. So long as the nascent working class was still completely without expression or organisation, and the peasants were still the dumb millions, the Indian bourgeoisie was the most progressive and objectively revolutionary force in India. They carried on work for social reform, for enlightenment, for education and modernisation against all that was backward and obscurantism in India. They pressed the demand for industrial and technical economic development.

But their faith and hope in British imperialism as their ally in this work were doomed to disappointment. British imperialism understood very clearly—more clearly than they did themselves—the significance of this progressive role, and the inevitable conflict that it would mean with the interests of imperialist rule and exploitation. Therefore from an early period the original patronage of the Congress turned to suspicion and hostility. Within three years of its foundation, the Viceroy, Lord Dufferin, its original inspirer, was speaking with contempt for the "microscopic minority" represented by the Congress. In 1887, (Mrs. Besant) relates in her book "How India Wrought for Freedom," a delegate attended the Congress" in denounce of his district officer and was called on to give a security of Rs. 20,000 to keep the peace." In 1890 the government issued a circular forbidding government officials to attend the Congress even as visitors. In 1900 (Lord Curzon) wrote in a letter to the Secretary of State: "The Congress is tottering to its fall, and one of my great ambitions while in India is to assist it to a peaceful demise" (Ronaldshay "Life of Lord Curzon, Vol. II. p. 151).

Frustration of their hopes in British imperialism was consequently the fate of the older school of Indian Nationalism. In his last years, Gokhale, the veteran leader of the Moderates, bitterly complained that "the bureaucracy was growing frankly selfish and openly hostile to National aspirations. It was not so in the past" (Official, *History of the Indian National Congress* 1935, p. 151).

As the failure of the old policy became clear, it was inevitable that a new school should arise, criticising the "Old Guard," and demanding a more positive programme and policy which should represent a definite breaking of the ties with imperialism. This new school, associated especially with the leadership of B.G. Tilak, came to the front already in the last decade of the nineteenth century, but was not able to play a decisive role until the situation became ripe in the following decade. Alongside Tilak, whose base was in Maharashtra in the Bombay Presidency, where the agrarian revolt had been most marked in the seventies, the best known of the newer leaders were Bepin Chandra Pal and Aurobindo Ghose in Bengal, and Lajpat Rai in the Punjab.

The new school termed themselves "Nationalists", also "Integral Nationalists" and "Orthodox Nationalists", and came to be widely known as "Extremists" in opposition to the "Moderates". It would be a mistake to regard these terms as the expression of a simple difference between a radical leftwing and a conservative-minded rightwing. In fact the situation bore a contradictory character, which reflected the still immature development of the national movement.

The starting point of the opposition leadership, as against the Old Guard, was undoubtedly the desire to make a break with compromising policies of conciliation with imperialism, and to enter on a path of decisive and uncompromising struggle against imperialism. To this extent they were a radical and potentially revolutionary force. But this desire was still a subjective desire on their part. There was no basis yet of the mass movement to make such a decisive struggle possible. Their appeal reached to the discontented lower middle class and to the hearts of the literate youth, especially to the poorer students and the new growing army of unemployed or poorly paid intellectuals, whose situation was becoming increasingly desperate in the opening years of the twentieth century, as it became manifest that there was no avenue of advance or fulfilment for them under imperialist conditions, and who were little inclined to be patient with the slow and comfortable doctrines of gradual advance preached by the solidly established upper-class leaders. Such elements can provide, in periods of social transition and the impending break-up of an old order, very considerable dynamic forces of unrest and potential revolutionary energy; but they are by the nature of their situation incapable of realising their aspirations, until they find their role in relationship to the mass movement, and can only seek satisfaction either in exalted verbal protest, or in anarchist individualist and ultimately politically ineffective forms of action.

Had the new leaders been equipped with a modern social and political outlook, they would have understood that their main task and the task of their supporters lay in the development of the organisation of the working class and of the mass of the peasantry on the basis of their social, economic and political struggle for liberation. But to have demanded such in understanding in the conditions of the first decade of the twentieth century in India would have been to demand an understanding in advance of the existing stage of social development.

Cut off from any scientific social and political theory, the new leaders sought to find the secret of the compromising ineffectiveness of the Moderate leaders in their "denationalised" "Westernising" tendencies, and concentrated their attack against these tendencies. Thus they fixed their attack against precisely those tendencies in respect of which the older Moderate leaders were progressive. Against these, they sought to build the national movement on the basis of the still massive forces of social conservatism in India, on the basis of Orthodox Hinduism and the affirmation of the supposed spiritual superiority of the ancient Hindu or "Aryan" civilisation to modern "Western" civilisation. They sought to build the national movement, the most advanced movement in India, on the basis of the most antiquated religion and religious superstitions. From this era dates the disastrous combination of political radicalism and social reaction in India, which has had such a maleficent influence on the fortunes of the national movement, and whose traces are still far from overcome.

The alliance of radical nationalism with the most reactionary forces of Orthodox Hinduism was signalised by Tilak when he opened his campaign in 1890 with a fight against the Age of Consent Bill, which sought to raise the age of consummation of marriage for girls from ten years to twelve years. This Bill was supported by Ranade and the older progressive national leaders. Tilak led a ferocious campaign against it, voicing the demands of the most reactionary forces of Hinduism. Later, he organised the "Cow Protection Society" (the sacredness of the cow, according to the principles of Hinduism. While originally explicable, like all religious observances, by the social needs of the period when the tenet arose, is today economically reactionary by its encouragement of useless livestock, leading to deterioration of livestock, and is also a dangerous source of friction with Muslims, who eat beef). National festivals were organised, not only in honour of Shivaji, the national hero of the Mahrattas, but equally in a religious form in honour of the elephant-headed God, Ganesh. In Bengal, the cult of Kali, the Goddess of destruction, was actively developed by some of the more ardent groups.

It is necessary to recognise the national patriotic purpose which underlay these religious forms. Beneath the protection of the religious cover widespread national agitation was conducted through annual festivals and mass gatherings, an organisation was developed with the formation of leagues under religious titles and gymnastic societies of the youth. Under conditions of severe imperialist repression of all direct political agitation and organisation, before the national movement had reached any mass basis, the use of such forms was justifiable. It was not a question, however, only of the formal cover, or of the historical form of growth of a political movement. The insistence on orthodox religion as the heart of the national movement, and the proclamation of the supposed spiritual superiority of the ancient Hindu civilisation to modern "Western" civilisation (what modern psychologists would no doubt term a compensatory delusion), inevitably retarded and weakened the real advance of the national movement and of political consciousness, while the emphasis on Hinduism must bear a share of the responsibility for the alienation of wide sections of Muslim opinion from the national movement.

These conceptions are so important for the subsequent development of Indian Nationalism—for they reappear during modern period in a more refined form in Gandhism—that it is worthwhile to analyse them with some care. For these conceptions are the expression of the belief that the path to Indian development and freedom lies, not along the line of social development, of overcoming old weaknesses and divisions and harmful traditions, but along the line of social retrogression, of stimulating and reviving the outlooks and relics of the past.

How this outlook arose we have seen. The Orthodox Nationalists saw the old upper-class Moderate leaders saturated with the "denationalised" outlook and methods, learning, social life and politics of the British bourgeoisie. Against this "denationalisation" or capitulation to British culture they sought to lead a revolt. But on what basis could they lead a revolt?

They were themselves, in fact, tied to the narrow range of the bourgeois outlook (socialism had not yet in practice made any contact with Indian political life at that time), and hence could not see with critical understanding the working of capitalism alike on its positive side and its negative side. In consequence they could not see that the so-called "British" culture they were denouncing was in reality the culture of capitalism: that the national movement, in so far as it was led by the bourgeoisie, could not yet transcend that basis: and that the only final progressive opposition to that culture could come from the working class. They could not, on the basis of experience then in India, have any conception of the rising working class outlook and culture which alone can be the alternative and successor to bourgeois culture going beyond it, taking what is of value and leaving the rest. Therefore, when they came to look for a firm ground of opposition to the conquerors' culture, they could only find for a basis the pre-capitalist culture of India before the conquest.

So from the existing foul welter of decaying and corrupt metaphysics, from the broken relics of the shattered village system, from the dead remains of court splendours of a vanished civilisation, they sought to fabricate and build up and reconstitute a golden dream of Hindu culture—a "purified" Hindu culture—which they could hold up as an ideal and a guiding light.

Against the overwhelming flood of British bourgeois culture and ideology, which they saw completely conquering the Indian bourgeoisie and intelligentsia, They sought to hold forward the feeble shield of a reconstructed Hindu ideology which had no longer any natural basis for its existence in actual life conditions. All social and scientific development was condemned by the more extreme devotees of this gospel as the conquerors' culture: every form of antiquated tradition, even abuse, privilege and obscurantism, was treated with respect and veneration.

So it came about that these militant national leaders of the people, devoted and fearless as many of them were, who should have been leading the people forward along the path of emancipation and understanding, away from all the evil relics of the past, appeared instead in practice as the champions of social reaction and superstition, of caste division and privilege, as the allies of all the "black" forces, seeking to hold down the antiquated pre-British social and ideological fetters upon the people in the name of a high-flown mystical "national" appeal.

The Orthodox Nationalists believed that in this way they were building up a mass national movement of opposition to imperialism. Only so can be explained that a man of the intellectual calibre of Tilak should have lent himself to such agitations as his campaign in defence of child-marriage or his Cow Protection Society.

But this policy was, in fact, no only vicious in principle, but mistaken in tactics. It not only inevitably weakened the advance of the political consciousness and clarity of the movement (nearly all the best-known leaders of Extremism moved later in varying degree to co-operation with imperialism, or to speculative abstraction from politics, and found themselves out of sympathy with the subsequent advance of the movement), but also divided the advancing forces. The programme of social reaction alienated many who would have been ready to support a more militant national policy, but were too clear-sighted to accept the reactionary and metaphysical rubbish which was being offered as a substitute for a left-wing programme. This division, tearing at the hearts of many of the best elements, was illustrated in the case of Motilal Nehru, a man of strong character who was one of the leaders of the Moderates in the fight against the Extremists, and of whom his son writes:

> "A man of strong feelings, strong passions, tremendous pride and great strength of will, he was very far from the moderate type. And yet in 1907 and 1908 and for some years afterwards he was undoubtedly a moderate of the Moderates and he was bitter against the Extremists, though I believe he admired Tilak.
>
> "Why was this so? . . . His clear thinking led him to see that hard and extreme words 'lead' nowhere unless they are followed by action appropriate to the language. He saw no effective action in prospect . . . . And then the background of these movements was a religious

nationalism which was alien to his nature. He did not look back to a revival in India of ancient times. He had no sympathy or understanding of them, and utterly disliked many old social customs, caste and the like which he considered reactionary. He looked to the West and felt greatly attracted by Western progress, and thought that this could come through an association with England.

"Socially speaking the revival of Indian Nationalism in 1907 was definitely reactionary."

(Jawaharlal Nehru, Autobiography, pp. 23-4)

In the practical struggle the Orthodox Nationalists while building on this religious basis for their argument could derive no weapon or plan of action therefore save the universal weapon of desperate, but impotent, petty-bourgeois elements divorced from any mass movement—individual terrorism. Even here the fruits of the very vague general religious incitation and exaltation, and formation of secret societies, were very meagre (despite the noisy outcry and publicity given to them by the horrified imperialist rulers, whose own methods of mass-extermination, later impressively illustrated at Amristar, were far more formidable), and played no part of importance until later the ripening of the situation for a new stage of struggle brought also this aspect to the front as an accompaniment.

When by 1905 the situation was ripe for a new stage of struggle, the remain weapon which was found was on which was remote from all the previous religious and metaphysical speculations, and bore an essentially modern and economic character—the weapon of the economic boycott. In the choice of this weapon, which was the only possible effective weapon at the time, was expressed the bourgeois character of the movement: and indeed support of this weapon was taken up by the Moderate leaders.

The forces which gathered for a new stage of struggle in 1905 reflected the wave of world advance at that time following the defeat of Tsarism by Japan (the first victory in modern times of an Asiatic over a European Power having its own profound repercussions in India) and the initial victories of the First Russian Revolution. The immediate issue which precipitated the struggle in India was the Partition of Bengal, then the centre of political advance in India, a plan devised by Lord Curzon and carried out under his successor. Against this partition, which aroused universal indignation, the boycott of foreign goods was proclaimed on August 7, 1905.

A rapid swing forward of the national movement followed. The 1905 session of the Congress still gave only conditional support to the boycott. But the Calcutta Congress in 1906, strongly under the influence of the Extremists, adopted a complete new programme, sponsored by the old Father of the Congress himself, Dadabhai Naoroji. This programme proclaimed for the first time the aim of Swaraj or Self-Government, defined as colonial self-government within the Empire ("the system of government obtaining in the self-governing British colonies"), support of the boycott movement, support of "Swadeshi" or the promotion of indigenous industries, and National Education. Swaraj, Boycott, Swadeshi and National Education became now the four cardinal points of the Congress programme.

A year later, in 1907, the Surat Congress saw a split between the Moderates, led by Gokhale, and the Extremists, led by Tilak. There is no doubt, on the evidence of an episode which long remained a controversial issue, that the Moderate leaders, fearing the growing influence of the Extremists, manoeuvred in a high-handed fashion to force the split. Thereafter the two sections developed in separation until the reunion in 1916: in 1918 the Moderates finally left the Congress to form the Liberal Federation.

The hand of government repression rapidly followed the new awakening for the movement. In 1907 was passed the Seditious Meetings Act, and a new and drastic Press Act followed in 1910 (the previous Press Act of 1878 had been repealed under the liberal administration of Lord Ripon in 1882. On the basis of a regulation of 1818 the method of deportation without trial was brought into play against the Extremist leaders. All this took place under the "Liberal" Lord Morley as Secretary for India. In 1908 Tilak, the man whom the government most feared, was sentenced to six years' imprisonment for an article published in his newspaper, and was held in prison in Mandalay until the month before the outbreak of the war of 1914. The arrest of Tilak led to a general strike of the Bombay textile workers—the first political action of the Indian proletariat, and hailed by Lenin at the time as a portent of the future. Most of the other prominent leaders were either sentenced or deported, or passed into exile to escape sentence. Between 1906 and 1909 there were 550 political cases before the courts in Bengal alone. Police action was carried out with great rigour; meetings were broken up: agrarian riots were ruthlessly suppressed in the Punjab: school-children were arrested for singing national songs.

As in the previous period repression was followed and accompanied by concessions to "rally the Moderates". The very limited Morley-Minto Reforms in 1909 gave a grudging extension to the system of representation initiated in the Indian Councils Act of 1892 by permitting a minority of indirectly elected members in the Central Legislative Council and a majority of indirectly elected members in the Provincial Councils; the Councils were advisory bodies and had no effective powers. The Moderate leaders, now in sole control of the Congress, seized the occasion of these reforms to proclaim their unity with the government: the new Viceroy, arriving in 1910, was received with a loyal Address: and when in 1911 the revision of the Partition of Bengal was announced in a Royal Proclamation, the spokesman of the Congress declared that "every heart is beating in unison with reverence and devotion to the British Throne, overflowing with revived confidence in and gratitude towards British statesmanship."

The revision of the Partition of Bengal in 1911 represented a partial victory of the boycott movement. The wave of struggle which had developed during the years 1906-1911 did not maintain its strength during the immediately succeeding years; but the permanent advance which had been achieved in the stature of the national movement was never lost. Despite all the limitations of the Extremist leaders of those pre-1914 years, they had achieved a great and lasting work: the Indian claim to freedom had for the first time during those years been brought to the forefront of world political questions; and the seed of the aim of complete national liberation, and of determined struggle to achieve it, had been implanted in the political movement, and was destined in the subsequent years to strike root in the masses of the people.

2. The Second Great Wave of Struggle, 1919-1922

It was the shock of the First World War with its lasting blow to the whole structure of imperialism, and the opening of the world revolutionary wave that followed in 1917 and after, which released the first mass movement of revolt in India.

Just as the awakening of 1905 reflected the world movement, even more so was this the case with the great mass movement which shook the foundations of British rule in India in the years succeeding 1917. This unity of the development of the struggle in India with the world struggle is of especial importance to realise, in view of the subjective and isolatisnist tendencies frequently prevalent in some of the conventional schools of Indian political thought to interpret profound movements simply in terms of the personalities or particular groups, which in varying degree sought or failed to give them leadership. There is no doubt that the transformation of the political movement in India from relatively restricted sections of the population to reach out to the masses of the people took place in the years succeeding 1917. But this transformation was not limited to India.

The war of 1914, following the lesson of the defeat of Russian Tsarism by Japan a decade earlier, completed the shattering of the myth of the invincibility of Western imperialism in the eyes of the Asiatic peoples. The spectacle of the suicidal conflict of the imperialist powers aroused hopes in the breasts of millions of the subject peoples that the hour of collapse of the existing Empires was at hand.

Imperialism took firm measures from the outset to hold the situation in hand, by the adoption of special legislation and powers, notably the Defence of India Act and by the imprisonment or internment of the most irreconcilable fighters or members of the revolutionary groups. In this task it was assisted in the earlier period of the imperialist war by the willing co-operation of the upper sections of the political movement. The Congress, under control of the Moderate leaders, proclaimed its loyalty and support of the imperialist war in resolutions adopted at each of its four annual sessions during the war, and even at the Delhi session in 1918 at the close of the war passed a resolution of loyalty to the King and congratulations on "the successful termination of the war". In return, the Congress was treated with official favour; the 1914 Congress was attended by Lord Pentland. Governor of Madras; the 1915 Congress attended by Lord Willingdon, Governor of Bombay, and the 1916 Congress by Sir James Meston, Governor of the United Provinces, the Government representatives being received with ovations. Representative Indian leaders in London at the time of the outbreak of war hastened to offer their support to the government. The Congress deputation then in London, including Lajpat Rai, Jinnah, Sinha and others sent a letter to the Secretary of State proclaiming their convention that "the Princes and people of India will readily and willingly operate to the best of their ability and afford opportunities of securing that end by placing the resources of their country at His Majesty's disposal" for "a speedy victory for the Empire". Gandhi, newly arrived in Lodnon from South Africa, in a reception at the Hotel Cecil, urged his young Indian friends to think "imperially" and "do their duty"; and in a letter from himself and other signatories to the Secretary of State offered his services:

> "It was thought desirable by many of us that during the crisis that has overtaken the Empire . . . those Indians who are residing in the United Kingdom and who can at all do so should place themselves unconditionally at the service of the Authorities. On behalf of ourselves and those whose names appear on the list appended hereto, we beg to offer our services to the Authorities".

His subsequent work in raising a volunteer ambulance corps of Indians in London is well known. On returning to India, he repeated his offer of service to the Viceroy, proposing to raise a corps of stretcher-bearers for service to the Mesopotamian campaign: the Viceroy replied, excusing him on grounds of health, and stating that "his presence in India itself at that critical time would be of more service than any that he might be able to render abroad". He responded to the Delhi War Conference called by the Viceroy in 1917, and as late as July 1918, he was conducting a recruiting campaign in which he urged the Gujarati peasants to win Swaraj by joining the army.

These demonstrations of "loyalty" by the Moderate leaders were regarded by British official opinion as an expression of gratitude and enthusiasm for the blessings of British rule. In fact, however, the calculation of these leaders, as they themselves subsequently explained, had been by these services to imperialism at war to open the door most rapidly to Indian self-government. Thus Gandhi declared, in his speech at his trial in 1922:

> "In all these efforts at service I was actuated by the belief that it was possible by such services to gain a status of full equality for my countrymen".

They were later to express their disillusionment.

The docility of the upper political leadership did not prevent the growth of mass unrest from the conditions of the war. The very heavy burdens of crippling financial contributions exacted from the poverty-stricken people of India for the service of the war, the rising prices and the reckless profiteering created conditions of mass misery and impoverishment, which were reflected in the unparalleled toll of the influenza epidemic at the end of the war, killing 14 millions. The growth of unrest was reflected in the Ghadr movement in the Punjab, and in mutinies in the army, which were suppressed with ruthless executions and sentences. In 1917 the Rowlatt Committee was appointed under a Judge of the King's Bench to enquire into "the criminal conspiracies connected with revolutionary movements in India" and recommend new repressive legislation.

The growing unrest began to find a reflection in the political movement, in which new stirrings appeared from 1916 onwards. In 1916 Tilak founded the Home Rule for India League. His campaign was joined by the English theosophist, Mrs. Besant, who sought to guide the national movement in channels of "loyalty" to the Empire and was later to take an active part in the fight against non-co-operation. Reunion between the Extremists and Moderates was achieved at the Lucknow Congress in 1916. Even more important, the plans for alliance between the Congress and the Moslem League (founded in 1905), which had been originally prepared at the Karachi Congress in 1913, reached fruition in 1916. One of the reason for this closer understanding was that Muslim feeling had been strongly aroused by the war against Turkey and the Muslim League Conference of 1915 had already revealed this discontent. In 1916 the Lucknow Pact of the two bodies reached agreement on a common scheme for reforms in the direction of partial self-government within the Empire (elected majorities in the Councils, extended powers of the Councils, half the Viceroy's Executive to be Indians), which became known as the Congress-League scheme. At the same time the aim was proclaimed of India becoming "an equal partner in the Empire with the self-governing Dominions".

This was the position when the rapid transformation of the world situation in 1917, following the Russian Revolution, affected the whole tempo of events and found its speedy reflection in the relations for Britain and India. The issue of national self-determination, and of the dissolution of the old Empires, was brought to the forefront by Russian Revolution in a manner highly embarrassing to the imperialist Powers on both sides. Within five months of the fall of Tsarism the British Government hastened to issue a declaration (known as the Montagu declaration, from the name of the Secretary of State at the time, but in fact planned and prepared by Curzon and Austen Chamberlain), which proclaimed the aims of British rule in India to be "the gradual development of self-governing institutions, with a view to the progressive realisation of Responsible Government in India as an integral part of the British Empire", and promising "substantial steps in this direction as soon as possible". The hasty character of this declaration was shown by the fact that only after it was made was the work begun to endeavour to find out what it was intended to do: the consequent Montagu-Chelmsford Report was only ready a year later; the Reforms (along the lines of so-called "Dyarchy" in the Provinces, or divisions of portfolios between British and Indian Ministers) were not enacted until the end of 1919 and only came into operation in 1920. By that time the whole situation in India had changed.

The Reforms were partially successful as with the Morley-Minto scheme a decade earlier, in creating a division in the upper-class national camp; but the support of the Moderates thus secured was of far less weight in the political situation at this more advanced stage of development. Mrs. Besant, presiding over the Calcutta Congress at the end of 1917, was able to secure the adoption of a resolution "that the Congress, speaking on behalf of the united people of India, begs respectfully to convey to His Majesty the King-Emperor their deep loyalty and profound attachment to the Throne, their unswerving allegiance to the British connection and their firm resolve to stand by the British Empire at all hazards and at all costs". But when the Report came out in the summer of 1918, a special session of the Congress at Bombay condemned the proposals as "disappointing and unsatisfactory". It was after this Special Congress that the principal Moderate leaders, other than Gandhi, left the Congress, later to found the Indian Liberal Federation, representing those bourgeois elements which wished to co-operate with imperialism. As late as December 1919, the Congress still went on record for acceptance of the Reforms: but this was only after a sharp division in which Gandhi, supported by Mrs. Besant, led the fight for co-operation, while the opposition was led, by C. R. Das. The final resolution reiterated the criticism of the Reforms, and the demand for "early steps to establish full Responsible Government in accordance with the principle of self-determination", but added, on the basis of an amendment moved by Gandhi, that "pending such introduction, this Congress trusts that, so far as may be possible, the people will so work the Reforms as to secure an early establishment of full Responsible Government".

Gandhi's view, as late as the end of 1919, in favour of co-operation and working the Reforms was expressed in an article in his weekly journal at the end of the year:

> "The Reforms Act coupled with the Proclamation is an earnest of the intention of the British people to do justice to

India and it ought to remove suspicion on that score . . . . Our duty therefore is not to subject the Reforms to carping criticism, but to settle down quietly to work so as to make them a success."

(M.K. Gandhi in *Young India,* December 31, 1919)

This declaration is important, since it was made after the Rowlatt Acts, after Amritsar and martial law in the Punjab—that is, after those issues which are subsequently declared to be the cause of non-co-operation—and thus shows that it was different calculations which led to the decision in the following year to inaugurate the non-co-operation movement.

For in fact, despite the still-continuing co-operation of the Congress, the whole situation in India had changed in 1919, and the basis for co-operation was disappearing from under the feet of the Congress. The year 1919 saw a mass wave of revolutionary unrest spread over India. Already the closing months of 1918 and the first months of 1919 saw the opening of a strike movement on a scale never before known in India. In December 1918, the Bombay mill strike began, which by January 1919, extended to 125,000 workers. The Rowlatt Acts, introduced in the beginning of 1919 and enacted in March, with the purpose to continue after the lapse of wartime legislation the extraordinary repressive powers of the government, for dispensing with ordinary court procedure and for imprisonment without trial, aroused widespread indignation as demonstrating the iron hand of imperialism beneath the velvet globe of Reform. Gandhi, utilising his South African experience, sought to organise a passive resistance movement against the Rowlatt Bills, and formed a Satyagraha League for this purpose in February. A hartal, or general day of suspension of business, was called for April 6. The response of the masses startled and overwhelmed the initiators of the movement. Through March and April a mighty wave of mass demonstrations, strikes, unrest, in some cases rioting, and courageous resistance to violent repression in the face of heavy casualities, spread over many parts of India. The official Government Report for the year speaks with alarmed amazement of the new-found unity of the people and the break-down of all official conceptions of Hindu-Muslim antagonism:

"One noticeable feature of the general excitement was the unprecedented fraternisation between the Hindus and the Moslems. Their union, between the leaders, had now for long been a fixed plan of the nationalist platform. In this time of public excitement even the lower classes agreed for once to forget the differences. Extra-ordinary scenes of fraternisation occurred. Hindus publicly accept water from the hands of Moslems and vice versa. Hindu-Moslem Unity was the watchword of processions indicated both by cries and by banners. Hindu leaders had actually been allowed to preach from the pulpit of a Mosque."

("India in 1919.")

Extraordinary measures of repression followed. It was at this time that the atrocity of Amritsar occurred, when General Dyer fired 1,600 rounds of ammunition into an unarmed crowd in an enclosed place without means of exit, killing (according to the official figures) 379 and leaving 1,200 wounded without means of attention, the object being, according to his subsequent statement, to create "a moral effect from a military point of view, not only on those who were present, but more especially throughout the Punjab"—i.e., to terrorise the population. It is a measure of the thick pall of repression which lay over India that any detailed news of this massacre only crept through even to the leaders of the Congress Committee four months later, and that for nearly eight months all news of it was officially suppressed and withheld from parliament and the British public. For diplomatic reasons, in face of agitation and a Congress enquiry, a committee had to be set up by the government to enquire into and condemn this outrage; but General Dyer received the plaudits (and a purse of £ 20,000) from the imperialists for his brave stand, and his action was officially approved by the House of Lords. Martial law was proclaimed in the Punjab; and the record of the wholesale shootings, hangings, bombing from the air, and extraordinary sentences perpetrated by the tribunals during this reign of terror, is still only available in fragmentary form from the subsequent enquiries.

"The movement", in the view of British official opinion, "assumed the undeniable character of an organised revolt against the British raj" (Sir Valentine Chirol, "India", 1926, p.

207) Gandhi too alarm at the situation which was developing. In view of sporadic cases of violence of the masses against their rulers which had appeared in Calcutta, Bombay, Ahmedabad and elsewhere, he declared that he had committed "a blunder of Himalayan dimensions which had enabled ill-disposed persons, not true passive resisters at all, to perpetrate disorders." Accordingly, he suspended passive resistance in the middle of April, within a week of the *hartal,* and thus called off the movement at the moment it was beginning to reach its height, on the grounds, as he subsequently explained in a letter to the Press on July 21, that "a civil resister never seeks to embarrass the government." This initial experience of "Satyagraha" (literally, "persistence in truth", used for the method of passive resistance) was to be subsequent repeated on an extended scale.

In December 1919, as has been seen, the Congress was deciding for working the Reforms, and Gandhi was urging that the task of the national movement was "to settle down quietly to work so as to make them a success." But the situation left no room for such dreams to be realised. The revolutionary tide of rising mass unrest, which had swept forward in 1919, was still advancing in 1920 and 1921, and was to be further intensified by the economic crisis which began to develop in the latter part of 1920. The first six months of 1920 saw the greatest height of the strike movement, with no less than 200 strikes involving one and a half million workers. Such a rising revolutionary tide made a mockery of the sage counsels of "settling down quietly". The President of the Congress declared at its special session in September, 1920:

> "It is no use blinking the fact that we are passing through a revolutionary period . . . . We are by instinct and tradition averse to revolutions. Traditionally, we are a slow-going people: but when we decide to move, we do move quickly and by rapid strides. No living organism can altogether escape revolting in the course of its existence."
>
> (Lajpat Rai, Presidential Address to the Calcutta Special Session of the National Congress in September, 1920.)

The analysis of the President of the Congress was in its essential point correct. The declaration of the spokesman of the

Congress was in fact a declaration that in the midst of "a revolutionary period" a leadership "by instinct and tradition averse to revolutions" was faced with the problem of leading the rising movement. Herein lay the contradiction of the post-war situation in India, as indeed in many countries at that time wherein the political movements had not yet reached a maturity corresponding to the opportunities unloosed by the war.

It was in this situation that in 1920 Gandhi and the main body of the Congress leadership (now deserted by the former Moderates) executed a decisive change of front, threw over co-operation with the Reforms, determined to take the leadership of the rising mass movement, and for this purpose evolved the plan of "non-violent non-co-operation". Henceforward the mass struggle was to be led by the Congress; but the price of the leadership was to be that the struggle must be "non-violent".

The new plan of non-violent non-cooperation was adopted at the Calcutta Special Congress in September, 1920. It was carried, not without opposition, by the alliance of Gandhi and Motialal Nehru with the militant Muslim leaders, the Ali brothers, at the head of the then powerful Khilafat agitation (in form the protest against the injustices of the Treaty of Sevres to Turkey, the leading Muslimi Power, but in practice the rallying point of Muslim mass unrest). The resolution proclaimed the policy of "progressive non-violent non-co-operation inaugurated by Mahatma Gandhi, until the said wrongs are righted and Swaraj is established." The policy envisaged successive stages, beginning with the renunciation of titles bestowed by the government, and the triple boycott (boycott of the legislatures, law courts and educational institutions) together with "reviving hand-spinning in every house and hand-weaving", and leading up at some future date to the final stage of non-payment of taxes. It will be seen that the immediate measures were measures of boycott to be adopted by the middle-class elements, officials, lawyers and students, with the only role for the masses the constructive task of "hard-spinning and hand-weaving"; the active participation of the masses, through non-payment of taxes (which inevitably meant a No-Rent Campaign), was reserved for later.

The boycott of the elections to the new legislatures, which took place in November, was markedly successful, two-thirds of the electors abstaining. The boycott of educational institutions had a considerable measure of success, masses, masses of students sweeping with enthusiasm into the non-co-operation movement. The lawyers' boycott was less successful, except for a few outstanding examples, such as those of Motilal Nehru and C. R. Das.

At the annual session of the Congress at Nagpur in December 1920, the new programme was finally adopted with practical unanimity. The greed of the Congress was changed from the previous proclamation of the aim of colonial self-government within the Empire, to be attained by constitutional means, to the new aim of "the attainment of Swaraj by peaceful and legitimate means." The organisation of the Congress was carried forward from its previous loose character to the machinery of a modern party, with its units reaching down to the villages and localities, and with a standing Executive ("Working Committee") of fifteen.

The new programme and policy inaugurated by Gandhi marked a giants advance for the National Congress. The Congress now stood out as a political party leading the masses in struggle against the government for the realisation of national freedom. From this point the National Congress won its position (a position at which the militant nationalists of the earlier years would have rubbed their eyes) as the central focus of the national movement.

But the new programme and policy contained also another element, an element alien to the mass struggle, an element of petty-bourgeois moralising speculations and reformist pacifism, which found it chosen expression in the innocent seeming term "non-violent". That term was intended by Gandhi to represent a whole religious-philosophical conception, preached by him with eloquence and devotion, akin in certain respects to older schools of Indian speculative thought but more closely related to and deriving from late Western schools of thought associated with Tolstoy, Thoreau and Emerson, which had their vogue and influence during Gandhi's earlier years in the West and in the formation of his thought. That same term was accepted by many of Gandhi's associates, who were far from sharing his philosophical conception, as an apparently common-sense rule of expediency for at any rate the earlier stages of struggle of an unarmed people against a powerfully armed ruling enemy. But in fact, as the subsequent experience of events and the ever-developing interpretation of that term were to demonstrate, that seemingly innocent humanitarian or expedient term contained concealed within it, not only the refusal of the final struggle, but the thwarting also of the immediate struggle by the attempt to conciliate the interests of the masses with the big bourgeois and landlord interests which were inevitably opposed to any decisive mass struggle. Herein lay the contradiction which was to lead to the collapse of the movement, despite great achievements, both in this first trial and in the extended trial a decade later, and the failure to win that speedy victory of Swaraj which was freely promised as the certain and rapid outcome of the new policy.

A great sweep forward of the mass movement followed the adoption by the Congress of the new militant programme of struggle against the government for the speedy realisation of Swaraj. Gandhi freely declared as a firm and certain prophecy (which, despite its naive character, was confidently believed by his followers in the flush of enthusiasm of those days) the rash promise that Swaraj would be achieved within twelve months, that is—for the date was definite—by December 31, 1921. He even went so far as to declare, at a conference in September, 1921, "that he was so sure of getting Swaraj before the end of the year that he could not conceive of himself as living beyond December 31, without having won Swaraj." (Subhase Bose, "The Indian Struggle", p. 84). However, he had still many years of political activity before him, though not yet the fortune of seeing the realisation of Swaraj.

Gandhi's plan of campaign was less clear than the date of victory. The official "History of the Indian National Congress" writes:

> "Mass civil disobedience was the thing that was luring the people. What was it, what would it be? Gandhi himself

never defined it, never elaborated it, never visualised it even to himself. It must unfold itself to a discerning vision, to a pure heart, from step to step, much as the pathway in a dense forest would reveal itself to the wayfarer's feet as he wends his weary way until a ray of light brightens the hopes of an all but despairing wanderer."

(Official "History of the Indian National Congress", 1935, p. 376.)

Subhas Bose relates his disheartenment when, as an eager young disciple in his first interview with the Mahatma in those fateful days of 1921, he sought to obtain "a clear understanding of the details—the successive stages—of his plan, leading on step by step to the ultimate seizure of power from the foreign bureaucracy", and filed to get an answer:

"What his real expectation was, I was unable to understand. Either he did not want to give out all his secrets prematurely or he did not have a clear conception of the tactics whereby the hands of the government could be forced."

(Subhas Bose, "The Indian Struggle 1920-1934", p. 68.)

Jawaharlal Nehru writes of the "delightful vagueness" of Gandhi:

"It was obvious that to most of our leaders Swaraj meant something much less than independence. Gandhiji was delightfully vague on the subject, and he did not encourage clear thinking about it either."

(Jawaharlal Nehru, "Autobiography", p. 76)

However, he explains:

"We all felt that he was a great and unique man and a glorious leader, and having put out faith in him we gave him an almost blank cheque, for the time being at least."

(Ibid., p. 73.)

The advance of the movement in 1921 was demonstrated, not only in the enthusiastic development of the non-co-operation movement, but in the accompanying rising forms of mass struggle in all parts of the country, as in the Assam-Bengal railway strike, the Midnapore No-Tax campaign, the Moplah rebellion in Malabar in the South, and the militant Akali movement against the government-defended rich Mohants in the Punjab.

Towards the closing months of 1921 the struggle leapt to new heights. The government, in deep alarm and anxiety over the whole situation, played their hoped-for Ace of Trumps against Gandhi by bringing in—not merely the Duke of Connaught, as earlier in the year—but the Prince of Wales Himself to tour India, not so much in any vain hopes of conciliating the people, as to test out the feeling of the population in relation to this royal image understood by every Anglo-Saxon expert of the mysterious East to represent the deepest object of veneration and adoration of the Oriental heart. The result exceeded their expectations—in the reverse direction. The *Hartal* all over India which greeted the Prince of Wales on his arrival on November 17 was the most overwhelming and successful demonstration of popular disaffection which India had yet known. The hostility of the people and the angry repression by the government led to sanguinary struggles, which Gandhi sought vainly to check and which led him to declare that Swaraj stank in his nostrils.

From this point the National Volunteer movement began to consolidate its ranks. They were still organised within the frame-work of the Congress or of the Khilafat movement on the basis of "non-violent non-co-operation"; but many wore uniform, drilled and marched in mass formation to organise *hartals* and the boycott of foreign cloth by picketing and peaceful persuasion.

The full force of government repression was turned against the National Volunteers. The Governmental Press, such as the *Statesman* and the *Englishman,* howled that the National Volunteers had taken possession of Calcutta and that the government had abdicated, and demanded immediate action. The government proclaimed the Volunteers illegal organisations. Arrests spread in thousands. Thousands of students and factory workers replenished the ranks of the Volunteers.

By the end of December all the best-known Congress leaders, except Gandhi, were imprisoned. Twenty thousand political prisoners filled the jails. At the highest point of the struggle, at the beginning of the following year, 30,000 were in jail. Enthusiasm was at fever heat.

The government was anxious and perplexed, and began to lose its nerve. If the infection of universal defiance of the government spread from the towns and began to reach the millions of the peasantry, there was no salvation left for British rule; all their guns and aeroplanes would not avail them in the seething cauldron of rebellion of 300 millions. The Viceroy proceeded, through the intermediary of Pandit Malaviya, to negotiate with the political leaders in jail. He offered legalisation of the National Volunteers and release of the prisoners in return for the calling off of civil disobedience. The negotiations proved abortive.

In this situation the Ahmedabad Congress was held at the close of the year, with Gandhi now almost alone in the leadership. Failing C. R. Das, the valiant leader of Bengal, who was to have presided and was in prison, Gandhi introduced an English clergyman at the opening of the proceedings to deliver a religious message to the Congress, who took the opportunity to deliver a homily against the burning of foreign cloth.

Amid enthusiasm the Ahmedabad Congress passed resolutions proclaiming "the fixed determination of the Congress to continue the campaign of non-violent non-co-operation with greater vigour . . .till Swaraj is established and the control of the Government of India passes into the hands of the people", calling on all over eighteen years of age to join the illegal National Volunteers, pledging the aim "to concentrate attention upon Civil Disobedience, whether mass or individual, whether of an offensive or defensive character", and placing full dictatorial powers for this purpose in the hands of "Mahatma Gandhi as the sole Executive authority of the Congress."

Gandhi was now Dictator of the Congress. The movement was at its highest point. Full powers had been placed in his hands to lead it to victory. The moment had come for the final trial of strength, for the launching of mass civil disobedience. The whole country was looking to Gandhi. What would he do?

In the midst of this ferment of national enthusiasm and hope one man on the Congress side was unhappy and alarmed at the development of events. That man was Gandhi. His, movement, the movement that he had envisaged, was not developing at all in the way that he had intended. Something was going wrong. This was not the perfect idyllic philosophic "non-violent" movement he had pictured. He had unchained a monster. Ugly elements were creeping in. Reckless men, especially among his Muslim colleagues, were even beginning to demand the abandonment of the "non-violence" clause. More and more openly, already in those closing weeks of 1921, when the tens of thousands of fighters were going to prison with his name on their lips, he was expressing his alarm and disgust, as in his revealing cry that Swaraj stank in his nostrils.

At Ahmedabad the retreat began. Not yet too openly, in the midst of that tense atmosphere of impending battle and expectant thousands. But the small signs were there. The Ahmedabad Congress was itself the historic moment and the ideal occasion for launching the call to mass civil disobedience throughout the country, the call to the final struggle and victory, for which the people were waiting. The Manifesto of the young Communist Party of India to the Ahmedabad Congress declared:

> "If the Congress would lead the revolution, which is shaking India to the very foundation, let it not put faith in mere demonstrations and temporary wild enthusiasm. Let it make the immediate demands of the Trade Unions its own demands; let it make the programme of the Kissan Sabhas (peasant unions) its own programme; and the time will soon come when the Congress will not stop before any obstacle; it will be backed by the irresistible strength of the entire population consciously fighting of their material interests."
>
> (Manifesto of the Communist Party of India to the Ahmedabad National Congress, 1921.)

The call to open struggle was not made at Ahmedabad. Instead, careful observers noted that all reference to non-payment of taxes had disappeared from the Ahmedabad resolution. The references to mass civil disobedience were hedged round with ifs and ans: "under proper safeguards", "under instructions to be issued", "when the mass of people have been sufficiently trained in methods of non-violence" . . . Then came the episode of the Republican Muslim leader, Hasrat Mohani, who wished to move a resolution defining Swaraj as "complete independence, free from all foreign control". Gandhi struck hard in opposition ("it has grieved me because it shows lack of responsibility"), and secured its rejection.

The Government of India, watching with straining eyes, saw the small signs at Ahmedabad and breathed a sign of relief. The Viceroy telegraphed to the Secretary of State in London:

> "During Christmas week the Congress held its annual meeting at Ahmedabad. Gandhi had been deeply impressed by the rioting at Bombay, as statements made by him at the time had indicated, and the rioting had brought home to him the dangers of mass civil disobedience; and the resolutions of the Congress gave evidence of this, since they not only rejected the proposals which the extreme wing of the Khilafat party had advanced for abandoning the policy of non-violence, but, whilst the organisation of civil disobedience when fulfilment of the Delhi conditions had taken place was urged in them, omitted any reference to the non-payment of taxes."
>
> ("Telegraphic Correspondence regarding the Situation in India", Cmd. 1586, 1922.)

What would Gandhi do? The Ahmedabad Congress had dissolved without a plan. All was left in Gandhi's hands. Like Parisian people in the siege of Paris, who endeavoured to comfort themselves with the belief that "General Trochu has a plan", the Indian people, under the hammer-blows of imperialist repression, looked hopefully to Gandhi to unfold his strategy.

Gandhi's action was peculiar. He waited a month. During this month districts approached him, pleading to begin a No-Tax campaign. One district, Guntur, began without permission. Gandhi sent an immediate note to the Congress officials to see that all taxes were paid by the date due. Then he decided to make a beginning with one tiny district where he had taken special care to ensure perfect "non-violent" conditions—the district of Bardoli, with a population of 87,000—or one four-thousandth the part of the Indian people that was awaiting his leadership to act. On February 1 he sent his ultimatum to the Viceroy to declare that, unless the prisoners were released and repressive measures abandoned, "mass civil disobedience" would begin—in Bardoli exclusively. Hardly had he done this when a few days later, news arrived that at a little village, Chauri Chaura in the United Provinces, angry peasants had stormed and burned the village police station and the unpopular village constabulary had perished in the flames. This news of the growth of unrest among the peasantry, the decisive question for the Indian revolution immediately determined Gandhi that there was no time to be lost. At a hasty meeting of the Working Committee at Bardoli on February 12, the decision was reached, in view of the "inhuman conduct of the mob at Chauri Chaura", to end, not only mass civil disobedience, but the whole campaign of civil disobedience through volunteer processions, the holding of public meetings under ban and the like, and to substitute a "constructive" programme of spinning, temperance reform and educational activities. The battle was over. The whole campaign was over. The mountain had indeed borne a mouse.

To say that the Bardoli decision created consternation in the Congress camp would be to fall short of any power of language to described the feeling that were aroused. The nearest approach for English readers would be the effect of the calling off of the general strike in 1926 as some parallel to India's Bardoli in 1922.

> "To sound the order of retreat just when public enthusiasm as reaching the boiling point was nothing short of a national calamity. The principal lieutenants of the Mahatma, Deshbandhu Das, Pandit Motilal Nehru and Lala Lajpat Rai, who were in prison, shared the popular resentment. I was with, the Deshbandu at the time, and I could see that he was beside himself with anger and sorrow."
>
> (Subhash Bose, "The Indian Struggle", p. 90)

Motilal Nehru, Lajpat Rai and others sent from prison long and indignation letters to Gandhi protesting at his decision. Gandhi coldly replied that men in prison were "civilly dead" and had no claim to any say in policy.

The entire movement, which had been organised on the basis of complete discouragement of any spontaneous mass activity and mechanical subordination to the will of one man, was inevitably thrown into helpless confusion and demoralisation by the Bardoli decision. Even Jawaharlal Nehru, who endeavours to defend the decision on the grounds that the movement would have otherwise got out of hand and certainly entered into the paths of violence and bloody struggle with the government, in which the government would certainly have won, admits that the manner of the decision:

> "brought about a certain demoralisation. It is possible that this sudden bottling up of a great movement contributed to a tragic development in the country. The drift to sporadic and futile violence in the political struggle was stopped, but the suppressed violence had to find a way out, and in the following years this perhaps aggravated the communal trouble."
>
> (Jawaharlal Nehru, *"Autobiography"*, p. 86.)

After the movement had been thus paralysed and demoralised from within, the government struck with confidence. On March 10 Gandhi was arrested and sentenced to six years' apportionment. Not a ripple followed in the mass movement. Within less than two years Gandhi was released. The crisis was over.

Great controversy had raged over the Bardoli decision and its bitter consequences for the national movement in the six years' subsequent ebb that followed. Defences have been put forward that the real cause and justification of the decision must be sought deeper than in the alleged issue of Chauri Chaura, officially given as the reason for the decision, and that in reality the time had come when it was essential to stop the movement because "our movement, in spite of its apparent power and widespread enthusiasm, was going to pieces"

(Nehru, "Autobiography", p. 85). It may be asked in what sense the movement was "going to pieces". If by this is meant that the reformist-pacifist control of the movement was weakening, this is undoubtedly correct. But this advance was inherent in the advance of the movement and the condition of its future victory (Nehru's assumption of the inevitability of the government's victory in the face of an all-Indian popular revolt would not have been as cheerfully assumed by the government). If, on the other hand, it might be taken to mean that the effective strength of the mass struggle had in reality passed its highest point and was weakening, such a claim would certainly not be correct, and is indeed not intended to be suggested even by the apologists. The clearest evidence of this is afforded by the government's own grave estimate of the actual forces of the situation three days before the Bardoli collapse. On February 9, 1922, the Viceroy telegraphed to London:

> "The lower classes in the towns have been seriously affected by the non-co-operation movement. . . . In certain areas the peasantry have been affected, particularly in parts of the Assam Valley, United Provinces, Bihar, Orissa and Bengal. As regards the Punjab, the Akali agitation . . has penetrated to the rural Sikhs. A large proportion of the Mohammedan population throughout the country are embittered and sullen . . . grave possibilities . . . The Government of India are prepared for disorder of a more formidable nature than has in the past occurred, and do not seek to minimise in any way the fact that great anxiety is caused by the situation."
>
> (Viceroy to Secretary of State for India, February 9, 1922, "Telegraphic Correspondence regarding the Situation in India", Cmd. 1586, 1922).

This was the government's picture of the situation three days before the whole campaign was cancelled by the Bardoli decision on February 12.[2]

The discipline of the mass movement and readiness for decisive struggle were shown by the example of Guntur, where, in despite of Gandhi's orders, through a misunderstanding the No-Tax campaign was inaugurated. Not 5 per cent of the taxes were collected—until Gandhi's counter-manding order came. On a word of command from the Congress centre this process could have undoubtedly been unleashed through the country, and would have turned into a universal refusal of land revenue and rent. But this process would have meant the sweeping away, not only of imperialism, but also of landlordism.

That these considerations were the decisive considerations behind the Bardoli decision is proved by the text of the decision itself. The text of the resolution adopted by the Working Committee at Bardoli on February 12 is so important as deserve reproduction, and repays careful study for the light it throws on the forces and contradictions of the Indian national movement.

NOTES

1. The touch of irony in the lavish encomia of British institutions customary with these older Congress leaders should not be missed. Thus it was Surendra Nath Banerjee who declared at the 1892 Congress: "We are the citizens of a great and free Empire and we live under the protecting shadow of one of the noblest constitutions the world has ever seen. The rights of Englishmen are ours, their privileges are ours, their constitution is ours. But we are excluded from them."

2. The impression of the government on the crisis of 1922 and their view that only Gandhi's calling off of the movement saved them was subsequently expressed by Lord Lloyd, then Governor of Bombay, in an interview:

   "He gave us a scare! His programme filled our jails. You can't go arresting people forever, you know—not when there are 319,000,000 of them. And if they had taken his next step and refused to pay taxes! God knows where we should have been!

   "Gandhi's was the most colossal experimenting world history; and it came within an inch of succeeding. But he couldn't control men's passions. They became violent and he called off his programme. You know the rest. We jailed him."

   (Lord Lloyd in an interview with Drew Pearson, quoted by C. F. Andrews in the New Republic, April 3, 1939.)

CHAPTER 3

The Rise of Indian Nationalism

An analysis has endeavoured to lay bare the situation and the forces preparing and making inevitable the advancing movement of the Indian people for liberation. The movement in its first stages necessarily takes on the character of a national democratic struggle of liberation from foreign rule alongside and intertwined with the struggle of the peasantry for liberation from the yoke of the landlords and moneylenders.

The history of the Indian National Movement is the history of the advancing consciousness and mass basis of this movement of national liberation, which began from a narrow circle of the rising bourgeoisie and professional strata with the most limited aims, and is only today, in the process of history, reaching out to its full stature and achievement, and preparing the way for a still more far-reaching social liberation.

1. Unity and Diversity

At the outset we are faced with a special question which is still frequently raised by the apologists of imperialism, although it has changed its form at different stages.

Is there a people of India? Can the diversified assembly of races and religions, with the barriers and divisions of caste, of language and other differences, and with the widely varying range of social and cultural levels, inhabiting the vast subcontinental expanse of India, be considered a "nation" or ever become a "nation"? Is not this a false transposition of

Western conceptions to entirely different conditions? Is not the only unity in India the unity imposed by British rule?

The approach to this basic question has gone through many stages. The older school of imperialists dismissed with contempt any conception of an Indian nation as an illusion. In the twentieth century the growing strength of the National movement led to a wider recognition, at any rate by the liberal imperialist school, of the existence of the Indian nation; and the alternative argument won favour that this development was a triumphant achievement and vindication of British rule and of the inculcation of British liberal ideals. In the most recent period, the emergence to political consciousness of the deeper masses of the Indian people, and the increasing indication of their multi-national character, has given a new aspect to this question. This aspect, which, correctly understood, in no sense runs contrary to the unity of India, has been distorted by the special propaganda of "Pakistan" with the theory of Hindus and Muslims as "two nations". Imperialist apologists have of course taken full advantage of this later argument.

The answer of the older school of imperialists, before the advancing strength of the nationalist movement had sicklied over their naive self-confidence with doubt, used to be very downright'.

"There is not and never was an India", was the form declaration of Sir John Strachey in 1888 in the spirit of the farmer at the zoo stoutly confronting the giraffe:

> "This is the first and most essential thing to learn about India—that there is not and never was an India or even any country of India, possessing, according to European ideas, any sort of unity, physical, political, social or religious: no Indian nation, no 'people of India', of which we hear so much."
>
> (Sir John Strachey: "India: Its Administration and Progress", 1888, p. 5.)

Sir John Seeley was no less deficit in his view:

"The notion that India is a nationality rests upon that

vulgar error which political science principally aims at eradicating. India is not a political name, but only a geographical expression like Europe or Africa. It does not mark the territory of a nation and a language, but the territory of many nations and many languages."

(Sir John Seeley, "The Expansion of England", 1885, pp. 254-7.)

"What is honour?" asked Sir John Falstaff, and answered: "A word. What is in that word honour; what is that honour? Air." In the same spirit of profound realism the struggle of the millions of India for freedom from foreign rule is proved our modern Sir John's a "vulgar error". So also the theorists of the Austrian Empire proved to their own satisfaction that Italy was a "a geographical expression".

Since the emphatic denials of those earlier days, which failed to arrest the advancing flood of the National movement, King Canute's courtiers have changed their tactics; and the alternative argument is now favoured that if there is an Indian nation, since all the efforts of imperialism, first to deny it, then to suppress it have failed, in that case it is self-evident that the existence of the Indian nation is a tribute to the achievement of British rule which has brought it into being. What degree of historical justification there is for this claim we shall consider in the next section.

But the argument from diversity, by implication either inferring the denial of Indian nationality, or intended to justify extreme slowness in its recognition, is still widely current. It is still to be found in all its glory in the principal propaganda piece of modern British imperialism about India, the "Survey Volume" of the Simon Report, which was produced in 1930 for wholesale circulation as a supposed information document for the general public on Indian questions. This memorable document of State begins by coolly declaring that "what is called the 'Indian Nationalist Movement'" (thus named as it were, with a pair of tongs) in reality "directly affects the hopes of a very small fraction of the teeming peoples of India." The brilliant insight of this judgement was immediately afterwards proved by the character of the civil disobedience movement of 1930-34 and the result of the elections of 1937. Thereafter the Report proceeds—always in the name of a purely scientific, impartial and objective presentation of pure facts for knowledge—to endeavour to terrorise the reader with the customary picture or the "immensity and difficulty" of the Indian "problem", the "immensity of area and population", the "complication of language" with no less than "222 vernaculars", the "rigid complication of innumerable castes", the "almost infinite diversity in its religious aspects", the "basic opposition" of Hindus and Muslims, this "variegated assemblage of races and creeds", this "conglomeration of races and religions", this "congeries of heterogeneous masses", and similar polite expressions in abundance.

The purpose of this approach is obvious. It is to create in the mind of the average unprejudiced reader the impression of the impossibility of any scheme of rapid self-government for India, and to induce him to draw as his main conclusion (in the words of H. W. Nevinson, reviewing the Report at the time in all good faith in a socialist journal):

> "The almost insuperable difficulty of constructing (not criticising) a constitution or form of government to suit a minor continent including 560 native Indian States (nominally independent), races of 222 separate languages, people of two main and hostile religions (168,000,000 Hindus and 60,000,000 Moslems in British India alone). 10,000,000 out casted or 'depressed' population, also called 'Untouchables'. . . . Everyone who thinks of India ought to know these bare facts to start with. If he does not, he should read Vol. I of the Report. If he neither knows nor reads, let him hold his peace."
>
> (H. W. Nevinson, review of the Simon Report in the *New Leader*, June 27, 1930.)

The fact that a conclusion of such a character should have been reached by a sympathetic left-wing representative like H. W. Nevinson in a "socialist" journal, and that this should have been typical of the reception, not merely in the official Press, but the almost the entire left Press at the time, liberal, labour or "socialist", all accepting this official propaganda at face value, is indicative of the success of this method of approach. For in truth this approach, despite all its air of impartial and statesman like recognition of unwelcome facts, is propaganda and barefaced propaganda. It is by no means a presentation of the elementary "bare facts" which everyone "ought to know" about India, but a conscious and deliberate selection of facts with a purpose, and a distortion even of all that underlies those facts. This official picture of India today, of the supposed "conditions of the problem", suppresses all that is cardinal for the real understanding of the present position of India, suppresses completely all facts of the imperialist exploitation of India, of the role of British finance-capital in India of the profits made by the British ruling class, of the methods of exploitation underlying the misery of the people, of the rising struggle of the masses (irrespective of racial or religious divisions) and of the method of suppression of that struggle by imperialism. These are the essential "bare facts". which an honest socialist journal or democratic journal should declare, everyone "ought to know" about India. Instead, this Report ("the Simon Commission . . . has done its work courageously and thoroughly . . appreciation must be expressed, so far as this first report is concerned, of the care with which Sir John Simon and his colleagues have approached their task. I doubt whether the most extreme Nationalist will be able to point to serious in—accuracies on major facts"—Fenner Brockway in the *New Leader,* June 13, 1930) dwells lovingly on whatever facts can be made to appear unfavourable to the people of India and to sustain the official principle of "Divide and Rule".

A citizen of the United States would be undoubtedly astonished if he were to read in a British Blue Book the following impartial survey of the condition of his country:

> "The sub-continent of the United States is characterised by the greatest diversity of climate and geographical features, while its inhabitants exhibit a similar diversity of race and religion. The customary talk of the United States as a single entitle tends to obscure, to the casual British observer, the variegated assemblage of races and creeds which make up the whole. In the City of New York alone there are to be found nearly a hundred different

nationalities, some of which are in such great numbers that New York is at once the largest Italian city, the largest Jewish city and the largest Negro city in the world. The contiguity of such diverse elements has been a fruitful cause of the most bitter communal conflicts. In the Southern States especially, this has led to interracial riots and murders which are only prevented from recurring by the presence of an external impartial power able to enforce law and order. The notoriety of the rival gangs of Chicago gunmen and of the Chinese hongs in New York have diverted attention from the not less pressing problems presented to the Paramount Power by the separate existence of the Mormons in Utah, the Finns in Minnesota, the Mexican immigration up the Mississippi and the Japanese on the West Coast: not to speak of the survival in considerable numbers of the aboriginal inhabitants."[1]

Yet this is the spirit in which the Simon Report approached its task of the survey of the condition of India.

Indeed, it is worth noting that similar profound analyses and "proofs" of the impossibility of unity of the American people were equally current in English expression on the very eve of the American Revolution. Lecky records in his history:

> "Great bodies of Dutch, Germans, French, Swedes, Scotch and Irish, scattered among the descendants of the English, contributed to the heterogeneous character of the colonies, and they comprised so many varieties of government religious belief, commercial interest and social type, that their union appeared to many incredible on the very eve of the Revolution."
>
> (W. E. H. Lecky, "History of England in the Eighteenth Century", Vol. IV, p. 12.)

And again:

> "A country where so large a proportion of the inhabitants were recent immigrants, drawn from different nations and possessing different creeds, where, owing to the vast extent of the territory and the imperfection of the means of communication, they were thrown very slightly in

contact with one another, and where the moneymaking spirit was peculiarly intense, was not likely to produce much patriotism or community of feeling."

(*Ibid*, p. 34.)

Burnaby, who travelled in the North American colonies in 1759 and 1760, wrote:

> "Fire and water are not more heterogeneous than the different colonies in North America. . . . Such is the difference of character, of manners, of religion, of interest, of the different colonies, that I think, if I am not wholly ignorant of the human mind, were they left to themselves, there would soon be a civil war from one end of the continent to the other; while the Indians and Negroes would with better reason impatiently watch the opportunity of exterminating them altogether."

Otis, the well-known American patriot, wrote in 1765:

> "God forbid these should ever prove undutiful to their mother-country. Whenever such a day shall come, it will be the beginning of a terrible scene. Were these colonies left to themselves tomorrow America would be a mere shambles of blood and confusion."[2]

The modern Die-Hards prophecies of the "dull roar and scream of carnage and confusion" (Churchill), if the British were to leave India, are thus only the stage-encore of a familiar recitation.

The democrat will accordingly be on his guard against these *interested* prophecies and presentations of facts on the part of the rulers of an empire on the eve of the victory of a National liberation movement.

The question of the historical degree of unity of India in the past can be left to the historians. It is worth noting that the modern school of historical research, even on the side of imperialism no longer endeavours to uphold the downright denial of the Seeleys and stracheys half a century ago, based on very slender information.

"The political unity of all India, although never attained

perfectly in fact, always was the ideal of the people throughout the centuries. The conception of the universal sovereign as the Chakravartin Raja runs through Sanskrit literature and is emphasised in scores of inscriptions. The story of the gathering of the nations to the battle of Kurukshetra, as told in the Mahabharata, implies the belief that all the Indian people, including those of the extreme south, were united by real bonds and concerned in interests common to all. European writers, as a rule, have been more conscious of the diversity than of the unity of India. Joseph Cunningham, an author of unusually independent spirit, is an exception. When describing the Sikh fears of British aggression in 1845, he recorded the acute and true observation that 'Hindustan, moreover, from Caubul to the valley of Assam, and the island of Ceylon, is regarded as one country, and dominion in it is associated in the minds of the people with the predominance of one monarch or one race'. India therefore possesses, and always has possessed for considerably more than two thousand years, ideal political unity. . .

"India beyond all doubt possesses a deep underlying fundamental unity, far more profound than that produced either by geographical isolation or by political suzerainty. The unity transcends the innumerable diversities of blood, colour, language, dress, manners and sect."

(Vincent A. Smith, "The Oxford History of India", 1919, Introduction, pp. ix-x.)

The present degree of unity is more important to consider; and here something needs to be said on those divisions which are so prominently displayed and emphasised by imperialist propaganda as obstacles to self-government and justifications for the necessity of continued British rule.

2. Questions of Caste, Religion and Language

Undoubtedly the Indian people has a heavy heritage of burdens, survival from the past, divisions and inequalities to overcome, as every people has its own inheritance and special problems. One of the strongest reasons for the necessity of self-government is in order that the progressive leaders of the people of India shall have the opportunity to tackle and solve these problems and carry forward the Indian people along the path of democratic and social advance. For the experience of the past half-century especially has already shown that, in the modern phase of imperialist decay (with the ending of the objectively progressive role of British rule in India in the first half of the nineteenth century), the offensive against these evils, such as untouchability, caste restrictions, communal divisions, illiteracy and the like is more and more actively led by the representatives of the Indian National movement, while imperialism has maintained an obstructive role against innumerable projects of reform, pressed and demanded by India's representatives, and has worked in such a way as to sustain and even intensify these evils.

A policy which in practice fosters and maintains the division and backwardness of a subject people, and in an underhand fashion works to intensify these evils, while in public it loudly proclaims these evils as a melancholy proof of the incapacity of the people for unity and self-government, condemns itself.

With regard to the communal or religious divisions, which constitute one of the most serious and urgent problems before the Indian people, it will be necessary to treat this question more fully. Proof will be given that in fact—in spite of official denials —this division has been undoubtedly fostered under British rule as a conscious act of policy. Indeed, the Simon Report itself was compelled to admit that the Hindu-Muslim antagonism is a special feature of the territories under direct British rule ("the comparative absence of communal strife in the Indian States today", p. 29), and has increased under British rule ("in British-India a generation ago . . . communal tension as a threat to civil peace was at a minimum. But the coming of the Reforms and the anticipation of what may follow them have given new point to Hindu-Muslim competition", p. 29). The communal problem will certainly never be completely solved till the imperialist ruler is removed.

The same applies to the Indian States or Princedoms, which owe their maintenance and continued existence entirely to the British protecting hand.

With regard to caste restrictions and untouchability, the outraged indignation of the representatives of the Carlton Club and of the colour bar (incidentally, the meaning of the original word for caste is "colour", and reflected the sense of superiority and exclusiveness of the Aryan invaders) against all caste restrictions and untouchability will undoubtedly be read with deep appreciation by the so differently placed scavengers in Britain, who, as is well known, are freely invited to the dining-tables of Mayfair. It is impossible not to appreciate the benevolent desire of the representatives of imperialism to magnify and multiply the numbers of the depressed classes and untouchables. A generation ago, before the political situation was so acute, the number of 30 millions was commonly given. Valentine Chirol, in his "Indian Unrest" in 1910, raised the figure to 50 millions. Anstey's "Economic Development of India", first published in 1929, boldly plumps, without evidence, for sixty millions; and this figure has been generally favoured on the platform and in parliament as the most impressive. The semi-official symposium "Modern India", published under the editorship of Sir John Cumming in 1931, hovers "from 30 to 60 millions." The Simon Report endeavoured to fix the figure at 43 million but at the same time pointed out that in the three Provinces of Bengal, United Provinces and Bihar and Orissa, covering 28 out of 43 millions, "the connection between theoretical untouchability and practical disability is less close, and a special investigation might show that the number of those who are denied equal rights in the matter of schools, water and the like is less than the total given for the depressed classes in those areas" (p. 41). Hence the total remains disputable.

The fight against untouchability has been led, not by the British Government, but by the progressive national movement. Indeed, the incident will be recalled when certain famous temples in Southern India, which had been traditionally closed to the untouchable were, under inspiration of Gandhi's crusade, thrown upon to them; and police were thereupon dispatched to prevent access of the untouchables, on the grounds that such access would be offensive to the religious sentiments of the population, which it was the sacred duty of the government to protect.

The British Government has certainly been concerned to organise a separate electoral roll of the untouchable or depressed classes, with guaranteed separate representation, in order to introduce a new element of division and weaken the National Congress. In this way the Scheduled Castes have been added to the lengthening list of separate electorates (though in the practical outcome this separate representation has been to a considerable extent nullified by the workings of the Poona Pact). But for the opinion of the untouchables themselves on this loving care, the evidence of the leader of the Scheduled Castes Federation, Dr. Ambedkar, who is accepted by the Government as their leader and spokesman, may be taken as given in his Presidential Address to the All-India Depressed Classes Congress in 1930:

> "I am afraid that the British choose to advertise unfortunate conditions, not with the object of removing them, but only because such a course serves well as an excuse for retarding the political progress of India."
>
> (Dr. B. R. Ambedkar, Presidential Address to the All-India Depressed Classes Congress, August, 1930.)

Dr. Ambedkar continued:

> "Before the British you were in the loathsome condition due to your untouchability. Has the British Government done anything to remove your untouchability? Before the British you could not draw water from the village. Has the British Government secured you the right to the well? Before the British you could not enter the temple. Can you enter now? Before the British you were denied entry into the police force. Does the British Government admit you in the force? Before the British you were not allowed to serve in the military. Is that career now open to you? Gentlemen, to none of these questions you can give an affirmative answer. Those who have held so much power over the country for such a long time must have done some good. But there is certainly no fundamental improvement in your position. So far as you are concerned, the British Government has accepted the arrangements as it found them and has preserved them faithfully in the manner of the Chinese tailor who, when given an old coat as a pattern, produced

with pride an exact replica, rents, patches and all. Your wrongs have remained as open sores and they have not been righted . . . .

"Nobody can remove your grievances as well as you can, and you cannot remove them unless you get political power in your own hands. No share of this political power can come to you so long as the British Government remains as it is. It is only in a Swaraj constitution that you stand any chance of getting the political power into your own hands without which you cannot bring salvation to your people."

The interests of the depressed classes and their liberation are inevitably linked up with the common national movement of liberation.

The crippling institutions of caste will only be overcome not by preaching and denunciation, but by the advance of modern industry and political democracy, as new social ties and common interest replace the old bonds. As Marx wrote:

"Modern industry will dissolve the hereditary division of labour, upon which rest the Indian castes, those decisive impediments to Indian progress and Indian power."

(Marx: "Future Results of British Rule in India", *New York, Tribune,* August 8, 1853)

The Census Reports already bear witness to the beginning of realisation of this prediction of Marx seventy years earlier:

"In places like Jamshedpur where work is done under modern conditions, men of all castes and races work side by side in the mill without any misgivings, regarding the caste of their neighbours."

(Bihar and Orissa Census Report, 1921)

Undoubtedly there are very heavy problems arising from the special disabilities weighing down the untouchables, outcastes or "Scheduled Castes", as they are now officially termed. It is these special disabilities and grievances which have provided the basis for the development of the Scheduled Castes Federation which has won a certain degrees of organised support in some areas. But the solution of these problems lies through the advance of the labour movement and democracy, and the fight of the democratic national movement for the removal of these disabilities, and not through separatist organisation of these groups as a sectional economic and political movement.

With regard to the division of languages, and the famous "222 separate languages", once again the hand of imperialist propaganda is visible in the fantastic exaggeration of this difficulty and in the character of the statistics provided for misleading the innocent. Different estimates can be provided from different authorities, ranging from 16 to 300. This variation already betrays the political interest behind the estimates. The 1901 Census reached a total of 147 languages. If we compare this with the 1921 Census, used by the Simon Report, we reach the interesting result that, whereas the population increased from 292 millions in 1901 to 316 millions in 1921 (without any influx of new foreign populations), the number of languages spoken increased from 147 in 1901 to 222 in 1921 (without the addition of any new or polyglot territory). Truly an amazing capacity of this Indian population to proliferate new languages in scores in a single generation.

But a more detailed examination will throw still further light on this heroic mythology of the "222 separate languages" which have so impressed non-Indian opinion.[3] Of these "222 separate languages" it will be found that no less than 134 belong to the "Tibeto-Burman sub-family". What is the character of these "languages"? Here light is thrown by the fuller list of 103 Indo-Chinese languages published in the "Imperial Gazetteer of India", 1909, Vol. 1, pp. 390-394. In this list of 103 languages we are given the number of speakers of each of these "different languages", and we find, for example, the following figures:

Language	*Number of Speakers*
Kabui	4
Andro	1
Kasui	11
Bhranu	15
Aka	26
Tairong	12
Nora	2

It is clear that the philosophical conception of language as a means of communication between human beings will have to be revised in the light of Andro, spoken by one person; Nora, with a grand total of two speakers, just scrapes through.

A detailed examination, which is only of value for exposing this type of imperialist propaganda, reveals (1) that the number of "languages" of the so-called Indo-Chinese family rose from 92 in 1901 to 145 in 1921: (2) that these "languages" are not spoken in India at all, but in outlying districts in the Himalayas and the Burmo-Chinese frontier: (3) that the vast majority of these are not languages at all, but either very minor dialects or names of tribes; (4) that out of the 103 "languages" included in the group, 17 are spoken by less than 100 persons; 39 by less than 1,000; 65 by less than 10,000; 83 by less than 50,000; 97 by less than 200,000. The only *language* in the group is Burmese.

Yet out of such materials is constructed the imposing total of "222 separate languages" which is trotted out on every imperialist platform, in every newspaper and in every parliamentary debate.

Since then the 1931 Census has reduced the total to 203. It is evident that some of the speakers of the languages spoken by one, two or four persons have unfortunately died in the interval, thus weakening by their thoughtless action the imperialist case against Indian self-government. The separation of Burma from India since 1937 will cause a still heavier mortality, since the majority of the languages (128), used to prove the divisions of the Indian people, belong to Burma. It is interesting to note that, in order to prove the case for the separation of Burma, the obstacle of the multiplicity of languages which had mainly been built up on the basis of Burma, suddenly disappeared and gave place to insistence on the essential unity of languages in Burma. "Though as many as 128 indigenous tongues are distinguished in the province", writes the Simon Report (p. 79), "nearly seven-tenths of the whole population—and the proportion is growing—speak Burmese or a closely allied language." So elastic are imperialist statistics in the interests of policy.

The problem of a common language for India is already on the way to solution on the basis of Hindustani (Hindi or Urdu according to the script), the official national language of the Congress, which is already either spoken or understood by the majority of the Indian people. "Hindu preachers and Mohammedan Moulvis", notes Gandhi ("Speeches and Writings", p. 398). "deliver their religious discourses throughout India in Hindi and Urdu, and even the illiterate masses follow them." Similarly in the Indian army, where there is no room for nonsense about "222 separate languages", military orders are given in Hindustani. The conception, often spread, of English as the supposed common language of *lingua franca* for India is a myth; after a century of English "education" only 1 per cent of the population can read and write English (3½ million out of 350 millions—1931 Census). As against this, "Hindustani with its various dialects accounts for over 120 million of people, and is spreading" (J. Nehru, "India and the World", p. 188). The problem of languages in India is in practice a problem of some twelve or thirteen languages ("there are twelve main languages in India", Sir Harcourt Butler in "Modern India", 1932, p. 8), of which the nine North Indian languages are extremely closely allied so that even the Census Report of 1921 had to admit:

> "There is no doubt that there is a common element in the main languages of Northern and Central India which renders their speakers without any great conscious change in their speech mutually intelligible to one another, and this common basis already forms an approach to a *lingua franca* over a large part of India."
>
> (Census of India, 1921, Vol. 1, Part I, p. 199.)[4]

It would have been more honest, if the Simon Report had reproduced this passage, instead of continuing to spread what it knew to be a misleading picture.

These special questions, which are commonly advanced as supposedly insuperable obstacles to the unity of the Indian people or to any rapid advance to self-government, and which all have their place as problems to be solved and soluble by national statesmanship, have only required this detailed treatment here in order to expose the type of fabricated imperialist propaganda which is built upon their basis and to warn democratic opinion outside India from being misled by this type of propaganda.

The real existence of the Indian nation, in the sense of the real unity of the Indian people in their struggle against imperialism, for their independence and right to build their own political future, will not be proved or disproved in the chambers of statisticians or the debating halls of parliaments. It will be proved, is being proved, and in the light of the experience of the past quarter of a century, we can say, has already been proved in the field of action. For, the problems of diversity or the multi-national character of the Indian people do not contradict this basic unity. They are problems which can only be settled and will be settled by the Indian people themselves.

3. Beginnings of Indian Nationalism

In the modern period the reality of the Indian nation can in practice no longer be denied, although the echoes of the old denial still survive. In consequence, with curious forgetfulness of the previous arguments which up to a generation ago so emphatically denied the Indian claim to national existence and dismissed India as "a geographical expression", the alternative argument is now in general favour with the more sophisticated spokesmen of imperialism, to the effect that if the Indian nation exists and has compelled recognition of the existence, then this must be regarded as the proud achievement of imperialism, which has brought Indian national consciousness into existence and planted the seeds of British democratic ideals in India; and even, by a kind of teleological anachronism, this is regarded as having been the real objective of British rule from the beginning.

> "The politically minded portion for the people of India . . . are intellectually our children. They have imbibed ideas which we ourselves have set before them, and we ought to reckon it to their credit. The present intellectual and moral stir in India is no reproach, but rather a tribute to our work."
>
> (Montagu-Chelmsford Report, 1918, p. 115.)

Thus, not the rising irreconcilable struggle of the Indian people against imperialism, but the beneficent handiwork of the philanthropic imperialist rulers themselves, is guiding the Indian people to national freedom. This is the picture which the modern cultured imperialists seeks to create in utterances for public consumption. The now much rarer public survivals of the old-fashioned type of utterance (such as the famous declaration of Joynson-Hicks that "we did not conquer India for the benefit of the Indians. I know that it is said at missionary meetings that we have conquered India to raise the level of the Indians. That is cant. We conquered India by the sword, and by the sword we shall hold it. We hold it as the finest outlet for British goods", or of Lord Rothermere that "many authorities estimate that the proportion of the vital trading, banking and shipping business of Britain directly dependent upon our connection with India is 20 per cent. India is the lynch-pin of the British Empire. If we lose India, the Empire must collapse—first economically, then politically") are now regarded in high official quarters as in bad taste, and tactically undesirable in an already sufficiently embarrassing situation.

There is no question of the change of tone in official utterance in the modern period. But the sceptical may be pardoned for enquiring whether the change of tone is not the reflection, rather than the cause, of the rising national movement.

Nothing could be more dangerous than for the new tone of official utterance to give rise to any illusions as to the iron realities to imperialist policy and power, or as to the intention of imperialism by every means at its command (the which means include the whole well-known armoury of deception as well as machine guns) to maintain that power. These realities it will be necessary to consider further when we come to the question of the latest British Plan.

The practical significance of this line of argument is evident. These patronising claims of modern imperialism, to take Indian Nationalism under its wing as its own foster-child, are by no means mere harmless self-delusions and self-consolations of a declining Power. The theory of imperialism, as a beneficent civilising system for helping forward and training backward peoples into national consciousness and eventual self-government (which has been termed in Marxist phraseology the theory of "decolonisation") was originally put forward by a school of socialist renegades and servants of imperialism like MacDonald—who subsequently showed his practical understanding of the "civilising" mission of imperialism by his reign of terror in India and imprisonment of 60,000 Indians, for the crime of demanding democratic rights. This theory has been taken up by the modern spokesmen of imperialism with a very practical purpose. For the practical conclusion to be drawn is that, in that case a "sane" and "constructive" Indian Nationalism will cease to regard imperialism as its enemy, will abandon the struggle for national independence and replace it by conciliation and co-operation with imperialism, and regard imperialism as its guide and tutor to lead the Indian people gently forward to a vague and undefined self-government, at a hypothetical future date at a tempo to be determined by the imperialists.

Is it correct to see Indian Nationalism as the offspring and outcome of British rule?

There is undoubtedly a sense in which this claim is correct, although certainly not the sense in which the makers of the claim intend it.

The Japanese invaders in China could no doubt claim, if they wished to do so, that by their invasion and aggression they were helping to forge the national unity of the people of China. And this claim would be objectively correct.

In the same way, insofar as modern Indian Nationalism has come into being and grown up in struggle against imperialism, imperialism can claim to be its precedent condition and starting-point, just as Tsarism was the starting-point of the victory of the working class in Russia, or Charles I of Cromwell.

This is not, however, what the modern imperialist apologists wish to imply. They wish to imply that the positive achievement of British rule not only by the political unification of India and the establishment of a modern centralised administration (here they are on strong ground), but also by the imposition of British legal and cultural institutions and the enforcement of an "Anglicised" education as the only medium of instruction for the tiny minority receiving any education inevitably laid the seeds of Indian Nationalism and implanted in the educated class English ideals of parliamentary government and democratic freedom. "English history taught the lesson of the gradual acquisition of popular liberties. English political thought as expressed by Brake and Mill reinforced the lesson. Educated Indians, essentially keen intellectually and readily stirred to enthusiasm, perceived a new revelation" (L.F. Rushbrook Williams, "What About India?" 1938, p. 105).

What is the measure of truth in this claim?

The democratic evolution of the modern age, which developed in many lands, including England as one of its earliest homes, is not the peculiar patent of England. Nor is it correct that it requires the alien domination of a country in order to implant the seeds of the democratic revolution. The American Declaration of Independence, and still more the great French Revolution with its gospel of Liberty, Equality and Fraternity, far more than the already ageing English parliamentary-monarchical compromise, were the great inspirers of the democratic movement of the nineteenth century. In the twentieth century, the Russian Revolutions of 1905 and 1917 have performed a corresponding role as the signal and starting-point of the awakening of the peoples, and especially of the awakening consciousness of the subject people of Asia and all the colonial countries to the claim of national freedom.

That the Indian awakening has developed in unison with these world currents can be demonstrated from the stages of its growth. It is worth recalling that Ram Mothan Roy, the father of Indian Nationalism in the first half of the nineteenth century, when he made the voyage to England in 1830, insisted, at considerable inconvenience, in travelling on a French ship to demonstrate his enthusiasm for the principles of the French Revolution. The National Congress, which was originally instituted under official inspiration as an intended instrument against the rising movement of the people and to safeguard

British rule, slept for twenty years, and first awakened from its slumbers in the great popular ferment and stirring after 1905, then again, when the revolutionary wave had subsided settled down to placid loyalist moderation, and once again, on a still more overwhelming scale swept forward with the world revolutionary movement after 1917.

The notion that India could have had no part in these world currents or pressed forward to the fight for national and democratic freedom, without the interposition of England, is fatuous self-complacency. On the contrary, the example of China has shown how far more powerfully the national democratic impulse has been able to advance and gain ground where imperialism had not been able to establish any complete previous domination: and this national democratic movement of liberation has had to struggle continuously against the obstacles imposed by imperialist aggression and penetration.

Did the Indian national movement arise because the educated class in India were taught by their masters to read Burke, Mill and Macaulay and to delight in the parliamentary rhetoric of a Gladstone and a Bright? So rungs familiar legend. The legend is too simple, and on a par with the derivation of modern France from the will of a Napolean of the Catholic derivation of Protestantism from the personal idiosyncrasies of Luther. The Indian national movement arose from social conditions, from the conditions of imperialism and its system of exploitation, and from the social and economic forces generated within Indian society under the conditions of that exploitation; the rise of the Indian bourgeoisie and its growing competition against the domination of the British bourgeoisie were inevitable whatever the system of education: and if the Indian bourgeoisie had been educated only in the Sanskrit Vedas, in monastic seclusion from every other current of thought, they would have assuredly found in the Sanskrit Vedas the inspiring principles and slogans of their struggle.

When Macaulay, on behalf of imperialism, imposed the system of Anglicised education, and defeated the orientalists his object was not to create Indian national consciousness, but to destroy it down to the very deepest roots of its being, in much the same spirit as the Tsarist methods of Rassification of the conquered nationalities of the old Russian Empire. His object was to train up a stratum of docile executants of the English will, cut off from every line of contact with their people. Nothing was farther from his thoughts then to implant the seeds of democracy. On that question his views were emphatic. It was Macaulay who declared: "We know that India cannot have a free government. But she may have the next best thing— a firm impartial despotism." The fact that this system of education, imposed in the interests of efficient imperialist administration, opened the avenues at the same time to the great stream of English democratic and popular inspiration and struggle, of the Miltons, the Shelleys and the Bytous-fighting against the selfsame types of tyranny, and even sometimes against the same figures of the ruling class oligarchy, the Pitts and the Hastings and the Wellingtons, as were enslaving and exploiting India—was a characteristic contradiction of the whole system of imperialism, conducted by the ruling class of a country, in which simultaneously the people were themselves pressing forward to their freedom. But this was a contradiction which was not foreseen at the time, and has never since ceased to be deplored by subsequent generations of imperialists,[5] who have done their best to avert its consequences by their increasing censorship of books to India.

There is no need to minimise the historical significance and achievement, for good and for evil, of British rule in India, or the contribution of that rule, however unwillingly or unconsciously, to the forces which have gone to mould the Indian nation. Marx showed, in those passages we have already had occasion to quote the two main elements of that achievement, whereby British rule in India, although actuated by "the vilest interets", nevertheless fulfilled the role of "the unconscious tool of history" in the development of India.

The first and most important achievement of the British conquest and exploitation of India was the negative achievement, or *destructive* role—the ruthless destruction of the foundations of the old order of society in India. Such a destruction was the necessary precedent to any new advance. It does not necessarily follow from this that such a destruction would have been impossible without the British conquest. On the contrary, there is some reason to judge that the traditional Indian society in decomposition at the moment of the British conquest was trembling on the verge of the first stage of the bourgeois revolution on the basis of its own resources, when the already matured British bourgeois revolution overtook it in the phase of disorder and transition, and was able to establish its domination. But in the actual historical record this destruction was the achievement of British rule.

The second achievement, less completely carried out, was the laying of the material basis for the new order by the political unification of the country, the linking up of India with the world market, the establishment of modern communications, especially the railways and telegraphic system, with the consequent first beginnings of modern industry and training of the necessary accompanying personnel with administrative and scientific qualifications.

These achievements could not in themselves bring either liberation or any improvement in conditions for the mass of the Indian people. They could only lay the material premises for both. But "has the bourgeoisie ever done more? Has it ever effected a progress without dragging individuals and people through blood and dirt, through misery and degradation?"

Rigid in their outlook, unsympathetic to all that was backward in Indian traditions, convinced that the nineteenth century British bourgeois and Christian conception was the norm for humanity, these early administrators nevertheless carried on a powerful work of innovation, representing the spirit of the early ascendant bourgeoisie of the period; and the best of there, like Sir Henry Lawrence, won the respect and affection of those with whom they had to deal. All tradition bears out the closer personal relations between British and Indian in that period. The deepest enemies of the British were the old reactionary rulers who saw in them their supplanters. The most progressive elements in Indian society at that time, represented by Ram Mohan Roy and the reform movement of the Brahmo Samaj, looked with unconcealed admiration to the British as the champions of progress, gave unhesitating support to their reforms, and saw in them the vanguard of a new civilisation.

The rising of 1857 was in its essential character and dominant leadership the revolt of the old conservative and feudal forces and dethroned potentiates for their rights and privileges which they saw in process of destruction. This reactionary character of the rising prevented any wide measure of popular support and doomed it to failure. Nevertheless, even so the rising laid bare the depth of mass discontent and unrest beneath the surface, and created an alarm in the British rulers, the tradition of which remains. "All India is at all times looking out for our downfall". Lord Metcalfe, Governor-General in 1835-36, had written already in the preceding period ("Papers and Correspondence", p. 116, quoted in J. L. Morison, "Lawerence of Lucknow", p. 55). "The people everywhere would rejoice, or fancy they would rejoice, at our destruction. And numbers are not wanting who would promote it by all means in their power."

After 1857 a transformation took place in British policy and the character of British rule. From this point British policy shifted its centre of gravity increasingly to winning the support of reaction in India against the masses; while its relationship to the new progressive forces, who represented the rising Indian bourgeoisie, passed from the former cordial closeness to coolness and suspicion, and even hostility, mitigated only by attempts here also to form temporary alliances of convenience against the masses. An abrupt end was made of the system of annexation of the Indian States into British India. Henceforth the remaining Princes were zealously preserved in possession of their puppet powers as allied "sovereign" rulers, with every form of degenerate feudal oppression and misrule protected, and even intensified, by their now completely parasitic role. The consequent political map of India was maintained as a senseless patch-work or petty principalities and divided administrations. In the most recent period these same Princes, now for the most part completely corrupt tools of their imperialist master, have been brought into the forefront of constitutional development as makeweights against the forces of national independence. The path of social reform was no longer actively pursued, but gave place more and more markedly to zealous protection of every reactionary religious survival and custom (the Age of Consent

Act of 1891 being almost the solitary exception in this later period). The Queen's Proclamation of 1858, while making a show of granting racial equality between Indians and English with regard to which the subsequent Viceroy, Lord Lytton declared that "these claims and expectations never can or will be fulfilled" emphasised the determination of the government to "abstain from all interference with religious belief or worship" and gave the pledge to the conservative forces of Indians society that "due regard will be paid to the ancient rights, usages and customs of India." The Royal Titles Act of 1876, by which the Queen was proclaimed Empress of India the following, what was declared by the Viceroy Lord Lytton, to represent the beginning of "a new policy by virtue of which the Crown of England should henceforth be identified with the hopes, the aspirations, the sympathies and interests of a powerful native aristocracy." From this period the methods of playing off Hindus and Muslims against one another, and of utilising other forms of sectional division, began to be more and more attentively studied, until, with the modern technique of communal electorates, this issue has been successfully brought into the forefront of Indian politics. At the same time an increasing alienation grew up since 1857 between the British rulers and the progressive elements in Indian society: all tradition on both sides agrees on the transformation of relations that took place.

Thus the change which developed in the general character of capitalism in Britain and on the world scale, from its earlier ascendant progressive period to a more and more reactionary and declining role and finally to full decay in the period of imperialism was accompanied by a corresponding change in the character of British rule in India. With the development into the final phase of modern imperialism or decaying capitalism this reactionary role has become especially emphasised.

On the other hand, while the objectively progressive role of the preceding phase of British rule in India was thus coming to an end in the later decades of the nineteenth century, new forces were growing up within Indian society. During the second half of the nineteenth century the Indian bourgeoisie was coming to the front. In 1853 the first successful cotton mill was started in Bombay. By 1880 there were 156 mills employing 44,000 workers. By 1900 there were 193 mills employing 161,000 workers. From the outset the new cotton textile industry was financed and controlled mainly by Indians; and it had to make its way against heavy difficulties. At the same time was appearing the new educated middle class, trained in the principles of Western education, developing as lawyers doctors, teachers and administrators, and advancing to the claims of nineteenth century democratic conceptions of citizenship. These beginnings, both in the field of capitalist industry and of the new Westernised intelligentsia, were still relatively small. But the new class was appearing, which was inevitably to find in the British bourgeoisie its overshadowing competitor and obstacle to advance, and was therefore destined to become the first articulate expression and leadership of Indian national claims.

The basic economic conflict between the new Indian bourgeoisie and the British bourgeoisie was already revealed, when in 1882 all duties on cotton imports into India were removed by the government in response to the demands of the Lancashire manufacturers against the rising Indian industry. Three years later the Indian National Congress was formed.

Finally, the growing impoverishment and desperation of the peasantry, consequent on the cumulative process of British capitalist penetration, were beginning to reach serious proportions by the second half of the nineteenth century and especially during its last three decades, and to find expression in mass unrest. It has already been noted that, while in the first half of the nineteenth century there were seven famines with an estimated total of 1½ million deaths, in the second half of the nineteenth century there were twenty-four famines with an estimated total of 28½ million deaths, and eighteen of these twenty-four famines fall into the last quarter of the nineteenth century. The Deccan peasant risings of 1875 were the warning signal of this growing unrest, and the anxiety of the government was revealed in the appointment of the Deccan Riots Commission in 1875, which conducted an exhaustive enquiry into the whole agrarian situation and the causes leading to the unrest, and of the Famine Commission in 1878.

Thus by the last quarter of the nineteenth century the conditions were now present, which had not existed in the first three-quarters for the beginning of the Indian National movement.

4. Risk of the National Congress

The Indian National Congress, the premier organisation and still the leading organisation of the Indian National movement, was founded in 1885.

The story of the origin of the National Congress has often been used to substantiate the claim of British imperialism to be the foster-patent of Indian Nationalism. In fact, however, the story of this origin and the contradiction of its subsequent history afford a striking demonstration of the strength of the forces of Indian Nationalism and of the inevitable growth of the struggle against imperialism.

As is well known, the National Congress, while arising from the preceding development and beginnings of activity of the Indian middle class, was brought into existence as an organisation through the initiative and under the guidance of an Englishman. More than that —what is less universally known— the National Congress was in fact brought into being through the initiative and under the guidance of direct British governmental policy, on a plan secretly prearranged with the Viceroy as an intended weapon for safeguarding British rule against the rising forces of popular unrest and anti-British feeling.

Yet no sooner had the legal existence of a national organisation, within whatever limited original intended bounds been thus authorised than its inevitable tendency as a focus of national feeling began to assert itself. From its early years even if at first in very limited and cautions forms the national character began to overshadow the loyalist character. Within a few years it was being regarded with suspicion and hostility by the government as a centre of "sedition". The subsequent developing mass movement of national struggle swept it forward, already in a first preliminary stage before the war of 1914 and still more decisively after it to the plane of semi-revolutionary mass struggle, vowing the aim of complete national independence, while the government proclaimed it illegal and sought to suppress it. Today the National Congress is the main focus of the organised millions of the national movement, and is widely seen as the alternative claimant to power in succession to British rule.

This history and development, defeating all the original claims of imperialism, is a testimony to the sweeping advance of the forces of the national movement and to the impossibility of confining those forces within the narrow channels which imperialism would have sought to mark out for them.

The origins of Indian Nationalism are commonly traced to the foundation of the National Congress in 1885. In fact, however, the precursors of the movement can be traced through the preceding half-century.[6] Reference has already been made to the reform movement which found expression in the Brahmo Samaj established in 1828. In 1843 was founded the British India Society in Bengal, which sought to "secure the welfare, extend the just rights and advance the interests of all classes of our fellow subjects." In 1851 this was merged into the British Indian Association, which in the following year presented a Petition to the British Parliament, declaring that "they cannot but feel that they have not profited by their connection with Great Britain to the extent which they had a right to expect", setting forth grievances with regard to the revenue system, the discouragement of manufactures, education and the question of admission to the higher administrative services and demanding a Legislative Council "possessing a popular character so as in some respects to represent the sentiments of the people." These earlier associations were still mainly linked up with the landowning interest; and indeed the merger by which the British Indian Association was formed, included the Bengal Landholders' Society. In 1875 the Indian Association, founded by Surendra Nath Banerjee, was the first organisation representative of the educated middle class in opposition to the domination of the big landowners. Branches, both of the more reactionary British Indian Association and of the more progressive Indian Association, were founded in various parts of India. In 1883 the Indian Association of

Calcutta called the first All-India National Conference, which was attended by representatives from Bengal, Madras, Bombay and the United Provinces. The National Conference of 1883 was held under the presidency of Ananda Mohan Bose who later became President of the National Congress in 1898; in his opening address he declared the Conference to be the first stage to a National Parliament. Thus the conception of an Indian National Congress had already been formed and was maturing from the initiative and activity of the Indian representatives themselves when the government intervened to take a hand. The government did not found a movement which had no previous existence or basis. The government stepped in to take charge of a movement which was in any case coming into existence and whose development it foresaw was inevitable.

The formation of the National Congress represented from the point of view of the government an attempt to defeat or rather forestall an impending revolution. The documents and memoirs available already prove this, although a complete account must await the opening of archives which are still secret and likely to be held secret until a change of regime.

The official founder of the National Congress was an English administrator, A.O. Hume, who had been in government service until 1882, when he retired and took up the work of the formation of the Congress. Hume in his official capacity had received possession of the voluminous secret police reports which revealed the growth of popular discontent and the spreading of underground conspiratorial organisation. The period of the seventies was a period of heavy famines and distress, and the growing unrest had been demonstrated in the Deccan peasant risings. The disastrous famine of 1877 coincided with the costly *durbar* at which Queen Victoria was proclaimed Empress of India and with the Second Afghan War. Unrest was met by repression. The freedom of the Press was removed by the Vernacular Press Act of 1878. In the following year the Arms Act left the villagers without even the means of defence against the raids of wild animals. The right of public meeting was cut down. The biographer of Hume writes:

> "These ill-started measures of reaction combined with Russian methods of police repression brought India under

Lord Lytton within measurable district of a revolutionary outbreak, and it was only in time that Mr. Hume and his Indian advisers were inspired to intervene."

(Sir William Wedderburn "Allan Occcasian Hume, Father of the Indian National Congress." 1913, p. 101.)

Sir William Wedderburn further explains the purpose of his intervention:

"Towards the close of Lord Lytton's viceroyalty, that is about 1878 and 1879. Mr. Hume become convinced that some definite action was called for to construct the growing unrest. From wellwishers in different parts of the country be received warnings of the danger to the government and to the future welfare of India from the economic suffering of the masses and the alienation of the intellectuals." (Ibid, p. 50)

The measures of repression preceded the foundation of the Congress with official blessing. The two processes were not contradictory but complementary. It was not until the potential revolutionary movement had been struck down that the way was judged open for the formation of a legal movement under docile leadership as the next step to "counteract the growing unrest". This double or alternative method of repression and conciliation of seeking to strike down the stubborn fighters and make an alliance with the "loyalist" moderates, is the familiar dialectic of imperialist statesmanship, destined to be many times repeated in the ensuing period.

What was the nature of the evidence which brought Hume to the conclusion that, as he wrote, "I could not then, and do not now, entertain a shadow of doubt that we were then truly in extreme danger of a most terrible revolution"? The evidence may be usefully given in his own words as expressed in a memorandum found among his papers: (the textual passages of the memorandum are given as quoted by his biographer, Sir William Wedderburn; the other passages are as summarised by his biographer):

"The evidence convinced me at the time—about fifteen

months I think before Lord Lytton left—that we were in imminent danger of a terrible outbreak. I was shown seven large volumes (corresponding to a certain mode of dividing the country excluding Burma, Assam and some minor tracts) containing a vast number of entries: English abstracts or translations—longer or shorter—of vernacular reports or communications of one kind or another, all arranged according to districts, sub-districts, sub-divisions and the cities, towns and villages included in these. The number of these entries was enormous: there were said at the time to be communications from over thirty thousand different reporters. Many of the entries reported conversations between men of the lowest classes, all going to show that these poor men were pervaded with a sense of the hopelessness of the existing state of affairs, that they were convinced that they would starve and die, and that they wanted to do *something*. They were going to do something, and stand by each other, and *that something meant violence.'* Innumerable entries referred to the secretion of old swords, spears and matchlocks, which would be ready when required. It was not supposed that the immediate result in its initial stages would be a revolt against our government or a revolt at all in the proper sense of the word. What was predicted was a sudden violent outbreak of sporadic crimes, murders of obnoxious persons, robbery of bankers, looting of bazars. In the existing state of the lowest half-starving classes, it was considered that the first few crimes would be the signal for hundreds of similar ones and for a general development of lawlessness, paralysing the authorities and the respectable classes. It was considered also that everywhere the small bands would begin to coalesce into large ones, like drops of water on a leaf; that all the bad characters in the country would join, and that very soon after the bands obtained formidable proportions, a certain small number of the educated classes, at the time desperately, perhaps unreasonably, bitter against the government would join the movement, assume here and there the lead, give the outbreak cohesion and direct it as a national revolt."

(Sir William Wedderburn, op. cit. pp. 80-81)

Hume established contact with the Viceroy, Lord Dufferin an experienced politician, in the early part of 1885, to place the situation before him. It was at this interview, in the headquarters of imperialism at Simla, that the plan of the Indian National Congress was hatched. The first President of the Congress, W. C. Bannerjee, has published his account of its origin:

> "It will probably be news to many that the Indian National Congress, as it was originally started and as it has since been carried on, is in reality the work of the Marquis of Dufferin and Ava, when that nobleman was the Governor-General of India. Mr. A. O. Hume, C. B., had in 1884 conceived the idea that it would be of great advantage to the country if leading politicians could be brought together once a year to discuss social matters and be upon friendly footing with one another. He did not desire that politics should form part of their discussion . . .
>
> "Lord Dufferin took great interest in the matter, and after considering it for some time he sent for Mr. Hume and told him that in his opinion Mr. Hume's project would not be of much use. He said there was no body of persons in this country who performed the functions which Her Majesty's Opposition did in England. . . . It would be very desirable in their interests as well as the interests of the ruled that Indian politicians should meet yearly, and point out to the government in what respects the administration was defective and how it could be improved and he added that an assembly such as he proposed shouldn't be presided over by the Local Governor, for in his presence the people might not like to speak out their minds. Mr. Hume was convinced by Lord Dufferin's arguments, and when he placed the two schemes, his own and Lord Dufferin's, before leading politicians in Calcutta, Bombay, Madras and other parts of the country, the latter unanimously accepted Lord Dufferin's scheme and proceeded to give effect to it. Lord Dufferin had mode it a condition with Mr. Hume that his name should use be divulged so long as he remained in the country.
>
> (W. C. Bannerjee, "Introduction to Indian Policy 1898.)

The traditional policy of liberal imperialism is here clearly expressed. Similarly the more recent historians of the early national movement have described the episode.

> "The years just before the Congress were among the most dangerous since 1857. It was Hume, among English officials, who saw the impending disaster and tried to prevent it. . . . He went to Simla in order to make clear to the authorities how almost desperate the situation had become. It is probable that his visit made the new Viceroy, who was a brilliant man of affairs, realise the gravity of the situation and encourage Hume to go on with the formation of the Congress. The time was fully ripe for this all-India movement. In place of an agrarian revolt, which would have had the sympathy and support of the educated classes, it gave the rising classes a national platform from which to create a New India. It was all to the good in the long-run that a revolutionary situation based on violence was not allowed to be created once again."
>
> (Andrews and Mookherjee, "Rise and Growth of the Congress in India". pp. 128-9.)

It will be seen that the official role of the National Congress as the organ of opposition to a "revolutionary situation based on violence" by no means dates from Gandhi: this principle was implanted in it by imperialism at the outset as its intended official role.

Hume's own conception of the role of the Congress may here be quoted:

> "A safety valve for the escape of great and growing forces generated by our own action, was urgently needed and no more efficacious safety-valve than our Congress movement could possibly be devise."
>
> (Wedderburn. op. cit., p. 77.)

Lord Dufferin's aim to build up through the Congress a basis of support for the government, by separating the "loyalist" elements from the "extremists", was very clearly set out in his speech on the demands of the educated classes in 1886, the year following the foundation of the Congress:

"India is not a country in which the machinery of European democratic agitation can be applied with impunity. My own inclination would be to examine carefully and seriously the demands which are the outcome of these various movements, to give quickly and with a good grace whatever it may be possible or desirable to accord, to announce that these concessions must be accepted as a final settlement of the Indian system for the next ten or fifteen years; and to forbid mass meetings and incendiary speechifying.

"Putting aside the demands of the extremists . . . the objects even of the more advanced party are neither very dangerous nor very extravagant . . . . Amongst the natives I have met, there are a considerable number who are both able and sensible and upon whose loyal co-operation one could undoubtedly rely. The fact of their supporting the government would popularise many of its acts which now have the appearance of being driven through the legislature by force: and if they in their turn had a native party behind them, the Government of India would cease to stand up, as it does now, an isolated rock in the middle of a tempestuous sea, around whose base the breakers dash themselves simultaneously from all the four quarters of the heavens."

(Sir Alfred Lvall: "Life of the Marquis of Dufferin and Ava," Vol. II, pp. 151-2.)

The calculation is here perfectly clear. And in the immediate outcome it looked at first as if it would be fully successful. The First Congress was most dutiful to imperialism: its nine resolutions cover only detail administrative reform suggestions; the nearest approach to a national democratic demand was the request for the admission of some elected members to the Legislative Councils. Mr. Hume's successful conduct of his flock was demonstrated in the closing episode recorded in the official report of the First Congress:

"Mr. Hume, after acknowledging the honour done him, said that, as the giving of cheers had been entrusted to him, he must be allowed to propose—on the principle of better late than never—giving of cheers and that not only three, but three times three, and if possible thrice that, for one the latchet of whose shoes he was unworthy to loose, one to, whom they were all dear, to whom they were all as children—need he say, Her, Most Gracious Majesty the Queen Empress.

"The rest of the speakers remarks was lost in the storm of applause that instantly burst out and the asked for cheers were given over and over."

It is a far cry from this servile beginning (the lowest depths, however, it will be noted of crawling boot-licking phraseology came, not from the Orientals, but from the Englishman) to the time when the Congress was a proscribed organisation, hunted down by the government and enlisting the devotion of millions of Indian fighters for freedom.

This twofold character of the National Congress in its origin is very important for all its subsequent history. This double strand in its role and being runs right through its history: on the one hand, the strand of co-operation with imperialism against the "menace" of the mass movement, on the other hand, the strand of leadership of the masses in the national struggle. This twofold character, which can be traced through all the contradictions of its leadership from Gokhale in the old stage to his disciple, Gandhi, in the new (the differences between these two deriving mainly from the difference of stage of the mass movement and consequent necessity of different tactics) is the reflection of the twofold or vacillating role of the Indian bourgeoisie, at once in conflict with the British bourgeoisie and desiring to lead the Indian people, yet fearing that "too rapid" advance may end in destroying its privileges along with those of the imperialists. This contradiction can only be finally solved in proportion as the national movement builds itself fully and completely on the masses and their interests in opposition to imperialism and to all those privileged interests which seek co-operation with imperialism.

NOTES

1. This admirable parody is from the pen of R. Page Arnot, in his article on "The Simon Commission Report" in the *Labour Monthly* for July, 1930, which is worth consulting.

2. These and other similar quotations can be consulted in the interesting appendix on "Contemporary India and America on the Eve of Becoming Free" in Major B. D. Basu's "Ruin of Indian Trade and Industries". Calcutta, 1935, pp. 254-67.

3. An exhaustive analysis will be found in the article on "Faked Indian Statistics as Imperialist Propaganda", published in the *Labour Monthly* of September, 1930, to which reference should be made for a fuller version of the facts given above.

4. It is amusing to note that as soon as the British exploiters have occasion to approach the question of the Indian market, the language difficulty, which for political purposes assumes such alarming proportions, is suddenly seen as easily manageable:

   "The language approach is not by any means so insuperable as would appear from the existence of scores of languages."

   (H.J. Fells, "The Indian Market: Hints to the British Exporter". *The Times Trade and Engineering India Supplement,* April, 1939.)

5. "The course and consequences of the measures taken by the British Government to promote Western education in India have been alternatively studied by the author of this volume. It is a story of grave political miscalculation."

   (Sir Alfred Lyall, G.C.I.E., Introduction to Valentine Chirol's "Indian Unrest", 1910, p. xiii.)

6. A fuller account of these precursors and early stages of the national movement will be found in C.F. Andrews and G. Mookerjee, "The Rise and Growth of the Congress in India", 1938.

CHAPTER 4

Andhra and the East India Company

The rule of the East India Company did not bring much good to the people. They suffered from all the evils of period of transition from an old to a new order. These evils were aggravated owing to the commercial outlook of the Directors of the Company in England and its influence on its servants in India. The shaking of the pagoda tree was the primary motive which influenced them all. To add to this were the corruption, lack of administrative experience, incompetence, and ignorance of the local language and customs which were characteristic of the Company's officials during the larger part of this period. Even the churchmen attached to the Company returned to England after making large fortunes by resorting to various illicit practices recognised and unrecognised. Ignorance of local language and customs resulted in the officials depending entirely on their Indian assistants in carrying on their administration. Very few of these assistants were honest. The large majority of them were unscrupulous. They were more interested in feathering their own nests than in giving disinterested help and advice to their superiors. How harmful their influence was is illustrated by what happened in Ganjam in the days of Collector Snodgrass, in Kistna when R. T. Porter was Collector with Sundaragiri Ramanuja Rao as Head Sheristadar, in Guntur during the five years following 1837 when the Head Sheristadar died and when the whole district was distracted by the intrigues and counter-intrigues of the subordinate revenue staff and in Nellore under Collector Travers.[1] The extreme dependence of the British Official on his

Indian subordinates was inevitable under the system that prevailed in the period of the Company's rule and very few among the officials were able to escape from it: and those who escaped. Major Munro for example, achieved great success as administrators. It is said that Munro was one of the first who carried to the work of revenue settlement a thorough acquaintance with the language and the manners of the people, an *undubashed* officer after several months that he could be captured.[2]

How troublesome the *poligars* were is brought out in a letter of the Court of Directors to the Madras Government written in 1803. It says: "We have derived little satisfaction from the perusal of the dispatches of Major-General Campbell commanding the troops in the provinces ceded to the Company by the Nizam in which we find the following paragraph:

> "Peace and order have been established by Military execution; but the country still swarms with armed men who have no employment. We can scarce doubt the disposition of the poligars, and their submission to authority can only be ensured by the presence of an active and respectable body of toops".[3]

All this indicates that those who held power in the past were not prepared to easily part with it and were determined to resist the new rulers.

Though as a result of the severe action taken against them, the *poligars* disappeared as a class, their spirit of revolt was not completely dead. So late as 1846—thirty years after Munro left the scene of his achievements— it found expression in the revolt of Narasimha Reddy who was connected through his mother with the *poligar* of Noosam, one of those who gave considerable trouble in 1801-02. He was in receipt of a paltry pension of Rs. 11-10-8 per mensem which was quite insufficient for his wants and he resolved on bettering his fortunes by means of a rebellion. He was able to secure the support of a large number of *cuttubadis*—the members of the village police who were then unfavourably disposed towards the government as a result of a move to resume their hereditary *inams*. A sanyasin to whom Narasimha Reddy was attached prophesied his success and this gave further encouragement to him. He produced a forged sanad from the "Raja of Golconda" calling upon all landholders to assist him in his designs.

He began his rebellion with an attack on the treasury at Coilcuntla which he got hold of successfully. Gradually his followers swelled to some five thousand and with them he marched across the Nallamalai hills in the direction of Cumbum. At Giddalur he was met by Lieutenant Watson defeated but he managed to retreat to Moondlapadu. By this time a stronger force under Captain Nott marched against him and he was once again defeated. He, however, took refuge in the jungles of the Nallamalai hills which could not be easily penetrated. For sometime his whereabouts were not known and it was presumed that he should have fled into the Nizam's territory where he had some sympathisers. Six weeks later he suddenly reappeared. The military promptly attacked him. This time he was captured and he was hanged at Coilcuntla and his body exposed in chains in a cage as a warning to other rebels. His insurrection proved more serious than that of any of the *poligars* in the days of Munro.[4]

The *poligars* of Chittoor district were as lawless and defiant as those of Rayalaseema. They enjoyed in practice a large amount of independence under the rule of the Nawabs of Arcot and they were now determined on fighting with a view to retain it. They began their rebellion when they were called upon to pay a heavier *peshcush* and also give up their customary right to collect *kavali* (watch and ward) fees from the villages.

The *poligar* of Naragati was the first to give serious trouble. He was arrested and kept under restraint by Stratton, the Collector. He was, however, released later on by the new Collector Cockburn on his promise to discharge all arrears. He not only did not keep his promise but also resumed his rebellious activities. A battalion was consequently sent to Chittoor but it did not take immediately to action as Cockburn wanted to give a chance to the *poligars* to come to a settlement. They refused to follow any conciliatory policy. In the engagements that followed several of their fortified strongholds were taken and destroyed. A battle was later on fought at

Nagapatla in which the *poligars* of Kallur, Pulicherla and Pullur were defeated (September 1803).

By this time most of the *poligars* were practically driven out of their homelands. They wandered about in jungles where they were beyond pursuit. Their followers pillaged the villages round about, seized the passes leading to Tirupati with a view to plunder the pilgrims. They also succeeded in surprising a party of sepoys stationed at a permanent settlement when the new revenue system was introduced into the district in 1802. With its introduction the period of revolts in the district came to an end.[5]

In the Krishna and Guntur districts there were fewer troubles from the Zamindars. In 1768-69 there was some trouble from the Zamindar of Ongole and his brother who created much disorder through the depredations he carried on. Military action was taken against them and they were put down. Similar troubles were created by one Padmanabha Rao, a relation of the Zamindar of Nuzvid, by Suraneni Venkatarayulu, who claimed some *mirasi* rights over four villages in the Nizamapatam Circar and by Kumara Viranna and his son Kumara Viresvara Rao of Palnad who had disputes with the government in regard to the pensions due to them. They did not, however, assume any serious proportions.[6]

In the Rayalaseema area ceded by the Nizam in 1800 the *poligars* occupied a position more or less similar to that of the Rajahs and Zamindars in the Northern Circars. They were the local military chiefs who held sway over some tract of country, subject to the condition of paying an annual tribute to the sovereign ruler and supplying him with military contingents whenever he called for them. It was not, however, in their blood to pay their tributes regularly. They generally defined the authority of the rulers and opportunities for such defiance increased in the second half of the eighteenth century when sovereignty over the areas passed frequently from one hand to another.

In 1800 there were rightly *poligars* in Rayalaseema. None of them was in a mood to recognise the authority of the British. They saw no reason for doing so. They had the natural impression that like the power of the Nizam, the rulers of Mysore and the Marathas the British power would soon pass away to be replaced by somebody else's. They evaded the demands for the payment of *peshcush* made upon them by Major Thomas Munro, the principal Collector of all the Ceded districts appointed to establish peace and order and make British rule effective. He issued a proclamation declaring that every chieftain who garrisoned a fort, maintained an armed force or revised contributions would be treated as a rebel and he promptly despatched military forces to seize the forts of the recalcitrant chieftains and compelled them to surrender.[7]

All the same there were several *poligars* who resisted his officers and when they were too weak to do this they absconded without paying rents and fled from one friendly chief to another in the hope of being able to raise adherents and hold on till the British were thrown out by another power like the Marathas. It took eighteen months for Munro to put down all of them.

Even then complete quiet could not be restored. There were occasional risings for a few more years before complete peace was established. In 1801, for instance, the panel or headman of Taranikallu in the Adoni Dvision took the law into his own hands, attacked the government officials in the Sub-Collector's Office and murdered some of them in open daylight. He then took refuge in his fort along with other insurgents and succeeded in beating off the troops sent against him. A larger force was then despatched and the place was taken by storm. The Patel was captured and hanged. In 1803 one Sultan Khan raised a body of a few hundred horses and suddenly appeared on the northern frontier of Cuddapah with the intention of capturing the town. Munro had previous information about the attack and made timely arrangements to meet it. In the affray that ensured Sultan Khan was defeated and captured.[8]

In 1804 there was a plot to seize Bellary fort and also a wide-spread conspiracy of capturing Adoni and establishing there the rule of Kudri Ulla Khan, son of Basalat Jang, the former Jagirdar of the place. But these did not materialise. In the same year there was a regular conspiracy among a number of *poligars* to capture the fort of Gooty and hand it over to the Marathas who were then carrying on a war with the British. The plot was discovered in time and the conspirators were arrested.

Revolts Against the British in Godavari (1785-1846)

The revolts of the Zamindars in the district of Godavari were neither so formidable nor so numerous as those in Ganjam. Most of the troublesome Zamindars lived in the hilly tracts. It was difficult to approach their mountain fastnesses on account of the unhealthiness of the climate and the impenetrable nature of the jungles that surrounded them. The chief of the Zamindars were those of Polavaram, Gutala and Kottapalli who were all members of the same family and the *mansabdar* of Rampa. Among those in the plains were the Rajahs of Peddapore. Pithapur, Kotaràmachandrapuram and Mogulturru. Besides the Zamindars there were the petty hill chieftains who for ages were accustomed to attack each other. To live in peace with their neighbours was not in their tradition.

The insurrections that broke out were due in the main to the resentment caused among the Zamindars and the *rentiers* by the steps taken from time to time by the government to collect tributes regularly and to prevent the accumulation of heavy arrears. Quarrels among kinsmen in which the government had necessarily to intervene to safeguard its financial interests were also responsible for some of the diturbances.

In 1785 Dasu Reddi, the *poligar* of the hill fort of Nagavaram, attacked and captured Gutala taking the young Rajah and his mother prisoners. At about the same time two usurpers named Koneti Tammadu and Viramallu Kannayya took possession of Kottapalli. Government sent seven companies of sepoys against them, put down the insurgents and restored the places to their original owners. Similar disturbances occurred in 1786 and 1787.

In 1788 the tribute from Gutala fell into arrears. In the interests of better management government placed this Zamindari under the control of the Dewan of Polavaram. This was resented by the mother of the young Rajah and she staged a *fituri* in 1790, with the help of some hill tribes. She was defeated by the troops sent against her and the Zamindari was handed over to her stepson Mangapati Devu, the Rajah of Polavaram.

In 1791 an insurrection was raised by one Jagga Razu in the Zamindari of Mogulturru as a result of intrigues of Bhupayya its *rentier*. A detachement of sepoys was sent against him and the disturbance was easily quelled. Bhupayya and another *rentier* Venkataramana Razu, however, continued their intrigues and they persisted in not paying the rents due from them. They were summoned to Madras and while they were there the government proposed to keep them in confinement. They somehow managed to escape and took refuge in Bhadrachalam in the territory of the Nizam. Bhupayya collected there a band of two thousand armed men, and entered the Zamindari. He was driven back and he once more took shelter in Bhadrachalam. He attempted no further incursions into Mogulturru.

Next came the trouble in 1799-1800 from Mangapati Devu of Polavaram and his brother Vijayagopala Devu. This was of a more serious and prolonged character. Mangapathi Devu failed to pay this tribute and the arrears went on accumulating. Government therefore ordered the sequestration of his estate until the arrears were cleared. Vijayagopala Devu had really no cause for discontent but he fell under the influence of evil advisers and became the first to start trouble. He fled in the first instance to Rampa and later on took refuge with one Linga Reddi, a hill chieftain who had a large number of Koya followers. It was here that he collected some forces and went about plundering the villages in Polavaram. In course of time Mangapati Devu also joined him. The revolt then took a more serious turn and government had to despatch a strong military force against the rebels. The fort of Polavaram was captured but Mangapati Devu escaped into the Nizam's territory. Martial law was proclaimed and a reward of Rs. 10,000 was offered for the apprehension of Mangapati. He renewed his attacks in 1800 with the help of Linga Reddi. Meanwhile, Vijayagopala surrendered himself to the government on promise of unconditional pardon. The military continued their operations until the insurrection was put down.

The estate was then handed over to a cousin of Mangapati Devu and it was with him that the English entered into head of a large body of armed followers and went on committing depredations. Behind him was one Naganna Dora, the Diwan of the Zamindar of Golugonda, "a double-faced scamp who had long fomented rising against government while vehemently protesting all the time his unswerving loyalty". After the arrival of George Russell in the district Jagannatha Raju disappeared for some time and reappeared in 1834. Troops were sent against him. He filled to Rampa in Godavari. The chief there gave him up and he was caught and hanged in 1834.[9]

Palkonda Zamindari also became an area of disturbance at about the same time. One of its earlier Zamindars, Viziaram Raj led a rebellion in 1793 which continued till 1796 when the government made over the Zamindari to his son Sitaram Raj. The latter died in 1798 and was succeeded by his brother Venkatapathi Raj. Viziaram who had been kept in confinement was subsequently set at liberty and he once more broke into rebellion in 1811 which could be suppressed only by the proclamation of martial law. Yenkatapathi Raj fell into arrears in regard to the payment of his tribute and orders were issued in 1828 to attack his lands. This led to a general rising but before the situation took a serious turn Venkatapathi Raj died. He left eight widows and two illegitimate sons behind him and was succeeded by Kurma Raj, the older of the two sons. As he was a minor the Zamindari was managed by one of the widows. Each of the ladies had, however, a faction of her own consisting of *mokasadars* and leaders of the hill-man. There was also a party which tried to oust Kurma Raj in favour of his brother. All this resulted in endless disturbances and in the plundering and burning of villages. In 1833 the insurgents made an attack on the Amin's office in Palkonda and collected themselves in the fort of Atsapavalasa in its neighbourhood. The commanding officer tried to attack them but he was beaten off. George Russell was then in the district. He went to Palkonda, proclaimed martial law, marched a detachment of sepoys against the rebels and captured all the ringleaders including the Zamindar. They were tried before a court martial. Some were sentenced to death and some were made state prisoners and all the members of the

Zamindar's family were removed to Vellore. Although Russel recommended the restoration of the Zamindari to a son of Venkatapathi Raj the government stood by the opinion of Sir Thomas Munro expressed by him when he toured the Circars in 1822 that, "No Zamindari once forfeited for rebellion should ever be restored. All estates falling in should invariably be kept and annexed to the Sirkar lands". A proclamation was issued forfeiting the Zaminidari and the forfeiture was subsequently made absolute and unconditional.[10]

In addition to the revolts of the Zamindars there were the *fituris* or outbreaks of the tribal people—the Adivasis in the hilly tracts. Golugonda was the scene of scveral such troubles. The first of them broke out in 1845 in protest against the confiscation of the Zamindari of Golugonda ruled by the ancient Bhupathi family. The hill Sirdars united together to restore the Bhupathi family to which they were attached and set up one Chinna Bhupathi as their Raja. They withheld their rents, barricaded the hills and burnt and plundered the villages in the plains. For three years they succeeded in defying the troops sent against them. In 1848 they laid down their arms on a promise of general amnesty and on the grant of allowances to Chinna Bhupathi and his brothers for their maintenance.

In the days of the mutiny in 1857-58 another insurrection broke out under the leadership of Chinna Bhupathi's nephew Sanyasi Bhupathi. This was, however, promptly put down. There were *fituris* in 1864-65-1886 and 1891 but they did not prove to be serious.

These and similar outbreaks among other Adivasis like the Savaras have shown that the tribal people constitute an inflammable element who can be easily roused to rebellion by any resolute and determined fanatic. This is illustrated by what happened in 1900 at Korravanivalasa in Gunpur area when four to five thousand hill people gathered round a Konda. Dora named Korra Mallayya who pretended that he was inspired and that he would drive out the English and rule the country himself. The *fituri* was easily put down.[11] The more recent exploits of Alluri Sitarama Raju illustrate this characteristic of the tribal people.

The situation, however, became unfavourable to him after some time and it was partly due to his own faults. He was not successful as an administrator. He was too simple-minded to understand the tricks played upon him by his courtiers. He was extravagant in his habits and the result was that his *peshcush* fell into arrears. When the arrears became heavy the Madras Government decided on taking severe steps against him even though the chief and council at Vizagapatam recommended more lenient measures and the Raja promised to pay the amount in instalments within a short period. Orders were passed sequestrating his whole estate and granting him a pension. On 2nd August, 1793, the fort of Vizianagaram was occupied by the English forces. The Zamindari was divided into three collectorates and officers were appointed to administer them.

Considerable difficulties were experienced by the Company's officers in carrying on the administration. The Raja had much influence in the district. The people sympathised with him. No one came forward to rent the taluks from the Government. Some Kshatriyas offered to take the estate on lease only from the Raja and to pay all the arrears. But the authorities were adamant. They felt that so long as the Raja was in the Zamindari no *rentier* would come forward to rent the lands. They, therefore, ordered him to leave Vizianagaram without delay and retire to Masulipatam on a monthly pension of Rs. 1200. It was a pittance unworthy of his dignity especially in view of the fact that the Company was paying to his ex-Dewan, Sitaram Raj, a monthly pension of Rs. 5,000.

On 11th May, 1794 the Raja proceeded a few miles but soon returned expressing his inability to go further. He was determined on making a bold stand and marched to Padmanabham, a sacred place half way between Vizianagaram and Bimlipatam. Most of his kinsmen joined him; some of the military retainers taken away from him also rallied to his standard. The government started some negotiations with him but these proved fruitless. Thereupon troops were sent against him on 10th July, 1794. A fierce battle took place at Padmanabham in which the Raja was defeated and killed. Round his dead body lay three hundred Kshatriya noblemen.

The battle has come to be known the "Flodden Field of Vizianagaram Rajputs" and it is commemorated in a Telugu *Prabandham.*

After the battle, Narayana Babu, the eight year old son of the Raja, took refuge in Kasipuram whose Zamindar was a rebel against the Company. A little later the boy fled to Makkuva further north in the hills. Thousands of armed men gathered round him. Several local noblemen collected rents from the ryots and organised measures to oppose the Company. The general commanding the English regiments felt that it would be difficult to coerce and fight the rebels in the hilly areas. Negotiations were once more started. The orders sequestrating the estate were withdrawn and this satisfied the followers of Narayana Babu. He was duly proclaimed Raja although he was compelled to pay four lakhs of rupees towards past arrears. The Zamindaris of Jaypore, Bobbili, Palaconda, Kurupam, Merangi, Sangamvalasa, Chemudu, Salur, Andra, Bhimavaram and Golugonda were handed over to their hereditary chieftains. In 1802 the permanent settlement was introduced and the *peshcush* from the Vizianagaram Zamindari was fixed at six lakhs per year. The battle of Padmanabham served for the time being as a warning to the other Zamindars and for some years there was no trouble from any of them.[12]

The lull was broken in 1830 when Virabhadra Raju of Kasipuram estate led a revolt as a result of some dispute regarding the pension payable to him by government. He collected a band of adventurers and set about laying waste the country around. The revolt assumed serious proportions by 1832 when George Russell arrived in the district as Special Commissioner. He sent a contingent of troops against the rebels. The troops burnt Kasipuram but Virabhadra Raju eluded capture owing to his superior knowledge of the hilly area in which he roamed about. The disturbances continued until martial law was proclaimed. In 1833 the rebel leader was betrayed by one of his own men, tried by court martial and sentenced to death. The government reduced the sentence to one of life imprisonment. With his capture the revolt came to an end.[13]

A similar disturbance was caused between 1832 and 1834 by one Jagannatha Raju who laid claim to the estates of Anakapalle and Satyavaram. He was at the neighbouring Zamindars and reduced their estates to a tributary condition. Among such estates were Jaypore, Sringavarapukoea, Madgole, Salur, Kotapalem, Kurupam, Anakapalle, Satyavaram, Golugonda, Palakonda, Andra, Regulavalasa, Koram, Thyada, Pachipenta, Sangamavalasa, Chamudu, Rajam and Narava. In 1765 he took over the estate of Bobbili after capturing its ruler, Chinna Ranga Rao, and imprisoning him in Vizianagaram. Having thus reduced the whole district of Vizagapatam including the hill areas he attacked the Parlakimidi estate in Ganjam. The Raja of Parlakimidi collected a Maratha force and met Sitaram Raj in battle at Narasannapeta but was severely defeated. He was thereupon compelled to go on a pilgrimage to the north and his estate was added to the Vizianagaram Zamindari for a time. Sitaram Raj next undertook an expedition against Rajahmundry, defeated the local Nawab and made the Rajahmundry Circar tributary to his brother.

When in 1766 the English became the rulers of the Circars as a result of their treaty with the Nizam he (Viziaram Raj) settled with them for an annual *peshcush* of three lakhs of rupees on the Vizagapatam estates excluding Parlakimidi. This proved to be of geat value to him as it secured for him their help in crushing a rebellion of hill Zamindars a little later.

The internal administration of Sitaram Raj was highly unpopular. He was harsh and cruel and exercised a sort of despotic control over Viziaram Raj, the ruler. The Kshatriya nobility were in resentment against him and they compelled him to retire in 1775. He then went to Madras, obtained the favour of the Governor and the members of the Council mostly through corruption, and got himself appointed Dewan against the Raja's will. In 1784 he was removed from the Dewanship.

Meanwhile, the Directors of the East India Company appointed a Committee of Circuit for the purpose of investigating into the political and financial conditions of the Circars as their expectation of getting large revenues from the area was not so far fulfilled. The Committee was appointed in

1777 but its work was suddenly stopped in 1779 by Sir Thomas Rumbold, the Governor of Madras. He issued orders to all the Zamindars that they should meet him in Madras for settling the amount of *peshcush* payable by them.[14] When Viziaram Raj received the order he replied that it would be inconvenient for him to leave his Zamindari and absent himself for a long time in Madras, that his circumstances did not permit him to incur the large expenditure on such a journey and that he was prepared to settle with the chief of the English factory at Vizagapatam the rent he should pay to the government. The Governor not only refused to accept that reply but also forced on the Raja the services of Sitaram Raj as Dewan. The Raja naturally resented such a treatment, but he was quite helpless in the matter until the Directors intervened in his favour and ultimately dismissed, Sir Thomas Rumbold on various charges of corruption in 1781. In a resolution which the House of Commons passed on 25th April, 1782, it expressed its indignation at the conduct of the Governor: "That the Governor did by menaces and harsh treatment compel Viziaram Raj, the Raja of Vizianagaram, to employ Sitaram Raj as the Dewan of the Zamindari, and that the harsh treatment and compulsive menaces to which the Raja was subjected were humiliating, unjust and cruel, and highly derogatory to the honour of the British nation". It is no wonder that in consequence of such treatment the Raja harboured feelligns of resentment towards the Company.

After the dismissal of Sir Thomas Rumbold the Committee of Circuit resumed its activities and recommended in its report that (1) the military forces at the disposal of the Raja which then amounted to 12,000 should be immediately disbanded; (2) in consideration of the unique position held by the Raja among the Zamindars of the Circars he should be allowed to have for his personal use 760 peons and 50 horses with an additional force of 2,000 to watch the passes leading from the hills to the plains; (3) the savings thus effected and amounting to nearly five lakhs should be added to the *peshcush* payable by him; (4) Jaypore should be made a separate Zamindari completely independent of Vizianagaram; and (5) the Zamindars imprisoned in the fort of Vizianagaram should be immediately released.

Viziaram Raj was prepared to accept most of the conditions but he was unwilling to pay higher *peshcush* as he was deeply involved in debt. Fortunately for him no action was taken for sometime on the recommendations of the Committee and the Dewan Sitaram Raj was removed from office.

Revolts Against the British in Vizagapatam (1794-1858)

Before narrating the history of the revolts of the Rajas and Zamindars in Vizagapatam district it is necessary to take note of certain general features which characterised the administration of the territories acquired by the East India Company. The one dominating motive of the Company's servants was to obtain the maximum amount of revenue irrespective of the hardships it caused to the ryots and the Zamindars. Money was the chief consideration in every transaction they undertook and money was required not only to secure larger profits to the Company but also to wage wars like the Mysore and Maratha wars. In the second place, the Company's servants of those days had no experience of administration. They were experts only in trade and commerce. It was the mentality of bargaining traders that they brought to bear on administration. To add to this was their ignorance of the language of the people, their customs and the traditional systems of land tenure. They were reduced to a state of complete dependence on the *dubashes* they employed for carrying on their administrative work and these were quite unscrupulous in their dealings. Ignorance led the Company's servants to resort to all sorts of experiments in their attempts to collect the maximum revenue—experiments like annual settlements, triennial settlements and quinquennial settlements. These frequent changes created much confusion and disorder which was partly responsible for the revolts of the Zamindars. Besides this they were strict in collecting the annual revenue or tribute to the last pie. They were not disposed to allow it to fall into arrears. This was something new in the experience of the Zamindars who were accustomed to leave much of their tribute unpaid and their discontent became all the more intense when the Zamindaris were threatened to be taken away from them for non-payment of tribute. This struck a blow at the hereditary basis of their estates. In the next place, the Company's servants showed no scruples whatever in utilising their political power for furthering their commercial objectives. This resulted in the oppression of the weavers and other craftsmen from whom they purchased articles for export. "The unscrupulous methods of loom collections, the tyranny of the *copdar* system and the unfair exercise of political power to coerce the unwilling artisans to work on unattractive wages compelled the weavers to forsake their trade and adopt different ways of life".[15] There were occasions when as a body the weavers refused to weave even an inch of cloth for the English merchants and went on a general strike. This was the utmost that they could do to give expression to their grievances. They had not the resources to do beyond this and take to rebellion. The Zamindars were in this respect in a better position with their forts and military retainers and they rose in revolt whenever they became discontented. Another feature which worsened the situation was the internal quarrels among the English chiefs and councils who had the responsibility for administering the conquered territories until Collectors were appointed in their place. Besides quarrelling among themselves they took their own line of action even in opposition sometimes to the orders issued by the Government of Madras. They allowed their territories to go from bad to worse obstructing every effort towards reform.[16] Finally, it should be noted that the Company was averse to the Zamindars maintaining large bands of military retainers. In its view it was objectionable from two standpoints. It led to the disturbances of peace and order in the country. It was also highly costly. The Company felt that if the military were disbanded the Zamindars would be in a position to pay a large amount of *peshcush*. The Zamindars were not in a mood to accept this view as their power ultimately rested on their possession of armed bands in their service.

It is features like these in the Company's policies and administration that provoked the revolts of the Zamindars and not merely their attitude of traditional defiance of all superior authority.

Of all the Rajas and Zamindars in Vizagapatam district Viziaram Raj, the Raja of Vizianagaram, was the biggest and the most powerful. He succeeded Anand Raj, the ally of Colonel

Forde and ruled from 1760 to 1794. In the days of anarchy that intervened between 1759 and 1767 his half brother the unscrupulous Sitaram Raj, who was his Dewan, engaged himself in a series of wars with him round failed, his Zamindari was declared to be forfeited to the government in 1815. Even then he did not yield. Troops were, thereupon, sent into his territory and some of the forts captured. He then gave himself up to the Collector and was finally sent to Chingleput as a state prisoner, a most lenient punishment for a person whose atrocities were of a monstrous character.

In 1818 Srikara Bhanj who had been in military custody since 1815 escaped and recovered possession of his Zamindari. On his promising to pay his tribute regularly he was formally reinstated in 1819. He continued to pay tribute till 1830-31 when he fell into arrears. He then retired and the government unwisely conferred the Zamindari on his son Dhananjaya Bhanj who had all along been a state prisoner.

Dhananjaya did not mend his ways. He did not pay the arrears of tribute. Some negotiations were started with him but before they were completed he rose in open rebellion. The government authorised the resumption of the Zamindari and to effect it troops were sent to the Goomsur country in 1835. Some of the forts were occupied but the situation did not improve. The Raja's followers harassed the English troops to such an extent that the Collector became inclined to restore the Zamindari to Dhananjaya. In his letter to the Madras Government he wrote" "The authority of government is only acknowledged in the District where the influence of the troops extends—the neighbouring Zamindars, the Hill Chiefs, the Sirdars, the inhabitants of the country as far as I can judge, and, in many instances I suspect, our own public servants are adverse to the downfall of the Goomsur family and the establishment of the power of government. We have been and are still obliged to draw every article of supply from a great distance. The enemy in small parties commit outrages upon such villages or individuals as are suspected of being friendly to our cause. . .

The object of all parties here is to have a Rajah and unless government is prepared to establish and maintain its power by force; I at present see little hope of a return to tranquillity but by establishing a Rajah". That such a letter was written by the Collector after nearly seventy years of British rule in the district shows how formidable was the resistance offered from time to time by the Zamindars of Ganjam.[17]

Dhananjaya fled to the Maliah hill tracts where he died in December 1835. His adherents continued the disturbances in alliance with the Khonds who were experts in methods of jungle warfare. The Madras Government then decided on a full scale military campaign and a war to the finish. George Russel was again appointed Special Commissioner with all the necessary powers and he was supplied with adequate forces for carrying on the operations.

Two campaigns were successively undertaken. In the first the strongholds at Kallada, Galeri and Durga Prasad below the Ghats were occupied and the country overrun in every direction. The rebels were compelled to take shelter in the distant hills. Then came the second campaign. For the first time English troops ascended the Ghats and entered the Maliah country. The troops met with opposition from the Khonds but they were gradually taught a lesson. The rebel chiefs who took refuge with the Bod Raja were captured and the insurrection came to an end by about the middle of 1837.

The Zamindari was forfeited to the government. The members of the Bhanj family were removed from the district and sent to Vellore. Almost all the ringleaders were captured and they were either hanged or transported. It was in this way that the rebellions and disturbances that had been prevailing in the country since 1768 were effectually stamped out and peace and security were restored.[18]

Among the other Rajas of Ganjam, who revolted from time to time against the British, Bhima Deo, the Raja of Vijayanagar and Pratapagiri, with his ten strong forts and five thousand armed forces proved to be the most formidable. His example was followed by his two sons—Main Deo and Jagannadha Deo.

One such disturbance occurred in 1856 and 1857. It was caused by the Savaras—a hill tribe—headed by Radhakrishna Dandasena of Gaiba. They plundered several villages and troops had to be sent into the interior of the Savara country before the disturbances could be suppressed. Dandasena was caught and hanged as a rebel in 1857. The reprisals of the troops upon this occasion and their penetrating into the heart of the Savara country had an excellent effect in preventing disturbances in the future.[19]

It is remarkable that on this occasion most of the Bissoyis and Doras in Parlakimidi gave most efficient assistance to the troops acting independently against the rioters.[20]

The Rajas of Goomsur proved to be as rebellious as those of Parlakimidi. They were the most ancient and the most powerful among the Rajas in Ganjam. They had numerous strong and will-protected forts and a band of eleven thousand military retainers in their pay. When the French got possession of the Circars from the Nizam they were among those who refused to pay tribute to the new rulers. Even after all others surrendered to Bussy in 1757, the then Raja of Goomsur continued to defy him. Bussy had to undertake an expedition against him before he could compete him to come to terms.

In the days of anarchy between 1759 and 1767 the Raja occupied twenty-three *hovele* (Government) villages outside his Zamindari and when the first English Resident arrived in Ganjam in 1768 it was only thirteen of them that he cared to surrender. Serious trouble began with the death of Raja Kissan Bhanj in 1773 and the accession of his son Vikrama Bhanj. The new ruler did not pay even a single rupee of tribute between 1773 and 1778. Troops were, therefore, despatched against him in 1778 and he was driven to take refuge in the Maratha country. From his exile he continued to forment disturbances and managed to recover some of the forts previously occupied by the English. The expedition was, therefore, renewed. He found it difficult to oppose the troops sent against him. He then proceeded secretly to Madras in 1779 and persuaded the Madras Council to reinstate him in his Zamindari in suppression of his brother Lachmana Bhanj. The disturbances, however, continued and the English Chief and Council decided to put Lochmana Bhanj in possession of the Zamindari on his agreeing to pay an annual tribute of a lakh of rupees. Though unable to meet his obligations he remained Raja till his death in 1788 when his son Srikara Bhanj succeeded to the Zamindari.

It was usual in·those days for revenue collections to be made through Sowcars who stood surety for the tributes payable by the Zamindars. The Sowcars were rapacious and exercised tyrannical control over the Zamindars. Srikara Bhanj suffered a great deal at their hands and in utter disgust he handed over his Zamindari to his son Dhananjaya Bhanj who proved to be one of the worst monsters of cruelty. Srikara Bhanj returned in 1795 from his pilgrimages and resumed control over the Zamindari. He withheld the payment of tribute from 1797 to 1800 excusing himself by saying that it was due to the ill-treatment and fraudulent practices of the Sowcars. That was also the time when the district suffered from the maladministration of Snodgrass, the Collector.

In 1800 he openly took up arms against the government and was joined by Mani Deo, the Raja of Vijayanagar and Jagannath Deo, the Raja of Pratapagiri. It was a formidable combination and a considerable body of troops had, therefore, to be sent against the rebels. The campaign went on for nearly two years. Some of the forts in Goomsur—Kallada and Durga Prasad—were captured and a proclamation was issued in 1801 formally deposing Srikara Bhanj and appointing his son Dhananjaya Bhanj, Raja in his stead. Srikara Bhanj continued to create disturbances from the hill tracts where he took refuge. All attempts to seize him failed. Conciliatory methods were then adopted and he was induced to agree to the accession of his son by allotting for his maintenance some Muthas (districts) in the Zamindari. All the same his presence in the area kept it in an unsettled and disturbed state. By 1808 Dhananjaya Bhanj acquired sufficient strength to compel his father to quit the area and go on a long pilgrimage from which he returned only in 1815.

Meanwhile Dhananjaya Bhanj indulged in all sorts of cruel atrocities including the murder of his own mother and the other wives of his father. When all attempts to bring was then in command of a Bengal battalion at Masulipatam to proceed against him. Colonel Peach did so, defeated him at Jalmar in May 1768 and compelled him to take refuge in the Maliah country (the highlands in the Eastern Ghats) attached to his Zamindari. To avoid complications and further disturbances, his son Gajapathi Deo was proclaimed Raja but real peace was not restored. Soon after the departure of Peach and his regiments, Narayan Deo returned and started intriguing with the Marathas in Cuttack and with Bhima Deo, the Raja of Vijayanagar. Though much did not come out of these intrigues troubles continued.

Gajapathi Deo did not prove more loyal to the British. In 1772 he fled from his estate and placed himself under the protection of Bhima Deo, the Raja of Vijayanagar. Apprehending danger the British Resident tried to induce him to return but failed in his endeavours. Thereupon the Zamindari was conferred upon his brother Jagannath Deo. Even than the situation did not improve. Jagannath Deo was no less rebellious than his predecessors. He was consequently dispossessed and Gajapathi Deo was reinstated. The latter repeatedly broke his engagements with the Company, disobeyed the orders of the Collector and neglected to pay his tribute. In 1798 the Collector issued a proclamation calling on the people not to help the Raja in his opposition to the Company and placed the Raja, his son and Dooga Rauz, a kinsman and a leader of importance, under a military guard. This led to a serious insurrection. Jagannath Deo, the Raja's brother, also joined the insurgents. It was with great difficulty that the brothers were separated and the uprising suppressed. Gajapathi Deo died in 1802 and was succeeded by his son Purushottama Narayana Deo. Jagannath Deo now disturbed the peace and continued his depredations till he was captured and imprisoned in 1804.

Purushottama Narayana Deo died in 1805. His son and successor Jagannath Gajapathi Narayana Deo was only twelve months old. The estate was therefore taken over by the Court of Wards, the actual management being left in the hands of Padmanabha Deo, the old manager. Partly due to the extreme unpopularity of this manager and partly due to the intrigues of Patta Mahadevi, the widow of Gajapathi Deo, disturbances broke out in October 1813. They assumed rather serious proportions and the Collector had to remove Padmanabha Deo as the only way out. In 1816 another rebellion broke out mostly through the intrigues of Padmanabha Deo leading to widespread anarchy. Martial law was proclaimed. The insurrection was suppressed with considerable difficulty.[21]

One of the causes of these frequent disturbances was the rebellious spirit of the Bissoyis and the peons (Doras). To add to this was the rivalry between Patta Mahadevi and Seviga Mahadevi (the mother of the minor Raja). Each of these had her own supporters among the Bissoyis and Doras. Both parties indulged in a sort of private war. Law and order completely broke down. Villages were burnt, Looting and plunder became the order of the day. Revenue could not be regularly collected and the tribute fell into heavy arrears. In 1829 the Zamindari was taken over by government and placed under the Court of Wards. Padmanabha Deo was again appointed manager. But this only led to the worsening of the situation. The Raja and his wife mobilised all the forces available and stood in opposition to the manager. One of the leading insurgents occupied a large part of the Zamindari and ran his own government.

It was then that the Madras Government realised the seriousness of the situation and appointed in 1832 George Russell Special Commissioner, with all the necessary powers—including the power to declare martial law—for suppressing the rebellion. He went to Ganjam with substantial military forces and took energetic measures for meeting the situation. He captured some of the important leaders in Parlakimidi. In 1833-34 he occupied the forts of Guma, Rayagudda and Jeringi. The last of these was considered by the people to be impregnable. Its fall consequently led to the weakening of the resistance offered by the rebels. Other forts were captured in course of time. Russell did not shrink from adopting harsh and even cruel measures to prevent any recurrence of the trouble. Several of the ringleaders were hanged, some were sent as prisoners to Vellore and some others were transported for life. The insurrection came to an end in 1834.

Though the Zamindari was not sequestrated, the Rajas the Bissoyis and the Doras were taught a lesson. Their rebellious spirit was extinguished and a period of peace dawned on the whole area disturbed only once or twice after 1834.

Revolts Against the British in Ganjam (1767-1863)

Several decades elapsed before the British could consolidate their hold over the territories they required. Formidable resistance was offered to them by the Rajas, Zamindars and Poligars who were the real power in those territories. The Rajas and Zamindars in Ganjam, Vizagapatam and other districts of the Circars were not mere farmers of revenue. They were hereditary chieftains with strong and well-garrisoned forts and large numbers of military retainers. Some of them traced their descent from well-known royal families which were in power several centuries earlier. They were always accustomed to defy authority and asserty their independent right to rule. They fought with each other and tried to extend their dominion at each other's expense. They never paid tribute which they owed to the *de jure* rulers of the country unless forced to do so.[22] In spite of their oppressive rule the people were attached to them. In the years of anarchy through which the Circars passed between 1759 and 1767 they were able to strengthen considerably their position. They were in no mood to surrender peacefully to the East India Company. They were determined to test their strength in fighting the Company and gave it constant and continuous trouble and the opposition offered by them was most formidable in Ganjam. Beyond the plains there were the hilly regions occupied by Savaras, Khonds and other tribal people. They often made depredations into the plains and it was customary for the Zamindars, to keep in their service numerous Bissoyis—hill chieftains—to prevent the hill people from breaking into the country and plundering it. These Bissoyis had their forts and they were assigned lands in return for the services they had to render.

From 1768 onwards for about fifty to sixty years no year passed without the use of the military by the British against several Zamindars before tribute due from them was collected. It was not only the bigger among them that refused to pay tribute but also the lesser ones. The threat of a general revolt became serious in 1780 when rumours broke out that the Marathas were about to invade Ganjam in large numbers from Cuttack and when news reached the Zamindars that Hyder Ali invaded the Carnatic and a French fleet under Suffren was on the Coromandel coast and when two French privateers actually made their appearance on the coast of Ganjam. The maladministration of the district by Thomas Snodgrass, who was Collector from 1791 to 1800, resulted in a general revolt of the Zamindars in 1800-1801. Isolated disturbances caused by the hill tribes went on till 1863 and it was only from that year onwards that the district became free from events of an untoward nature. These revolts of the Rajas are, though on a miniature scale, similar to the wars waged by the Rajputs against the Sultans of Delhi and the Mughal Emperors with a view to preserve their independence.

Some of these revolts deserve a more detailed treatment.

Among the more formidable of the rebels were the Rajas of Parlakimidi. They claimed their descent from the Gajapathis of Orissa. When the British acquired the Circars from the Nizam in 1766, Narayan Deo was the Raja. In the treaty between the Nizam and the British concluded in 1768 he was prominently mentioned. "*Narraindoo*, one of the Zamindars of the Circars of Chicacole, has lately raised disturbances in the *Itchapore* country, and refused to pay his rents or obedience to the Company; the Nabob *Ausuph Jah* agrees .... to write letters not only to Narraindoo, but to all the Zamindars in the Circars acquainting them, that they are in future to regard the English Company as their sovereign and to pay their rents and obedience to the said Company. . . . without raising any troubles or disturbances."[23]

The Growth of Anti-British Sentiments in Hyderabad

The early connection of the Nizams with the French in the middle of the 18th century resulted in the establishment of a colony of the French and those of other Europeans in Hyderabad about the time. The French influence persisted till the beginning of the 19th century. The association of the leading chiefs and noblemen of Hyderabad with the French had its effect in the promotion of Hyderabad's interest in the European way of life. The English also started dealings with the Nizam and his court from as early as 1759 A.D. The first envoy of the East India Company to the court of the Nizam was Mr. Holland, who reached Hyderabad in 1779 A.D. This association with the English became stronger, at the end of the 18th century when British influence became paramount in Hyderabad. The relics of influence in Hyderabad can be seen in places like the

Troop Bazars, the Gun Foundry, Mons. Raymond's tomb and the remains of the barracks once occupied by the French troops.

The Residents of the East India Company for a long time occupied the garden-house of Mir Alam. This was later on replaced by a well-built Residency in 1806 A.D., which was described as artistic, magnificent and perfectly English in its compforts by Sir James Mackintosh, who visited Hyderabad in December 1808 A.D. The Residency attracted a small colony of Europeans, East Asians, native Christians and the business people from the city. A small colony sprang up in Secunderabad, which had come into existence in 1805 A.D. Christian Missionaries also established themselves in these areas. A small beginning is also discernible in the field of education in the earlier half of the 19th century. The St. George's Grammar School, the oldest English School in Hyderabad, was established in the year 1834 A.D. and was attracting a number of pupils from the city. A medical school was started by the Resident at Bolarum in 1839 but was later closed and shifted on the Nizam's recommendation to the Residency in 1846 A.D. Speaking of this school, the administration report of Hyderabad for 1869-1870 A.D. compiled by C.B. Saunders, the then Resident, says as follows[24]:

DISPENSARIES

Hyderabad Medical School

The centre, or heart, of the whole dispensary system under the native Government is the Hyderabad Medical School, an institution which has long been to the Nizam's medical department all that the Engineering College described above is intended to prove towards that of public works.

Its aim is a high one, namely, the education of qualified practitioners of medicine and surgery, capable of assuming independent medical charges in the service of the Nizam's Government, or of entering upon private practice in different parts of the Hyderabad country.

The school itself is situated, like the Engineering College, outside the city, and indeed close to the Residency.

It has been presided over, even since its first establishment in the year 1846, by the Residency Surgeon, who receives a distant salary from His Highness's Government in his capacity of Superintendent or Principal of this school. He has three assistants in the work of tuition, all of whom are servants of the Nizam.

The link thus existing between the school and the Residency has been a most advantageous one. At the same time, the institution itself pertains entirely to the native government, and no interference in its management has ever proceeded from the Resident. Much of its success is due to the sustained personal interest which has been taken in it by Sir Salar Jung himself, and much also to the thoughtful and earnest advisers with respect to its administration whom he and his predecessors have found in its successive Superintendents. Among these indeed have been several of the most eminent past or present members of the Madras Medical Service. Dr. W. Maclean, for example, who enjoys, I am told, a European reputation as Principal of the Netley College in England; and Dr. George Smith, now Principal of the Madras Medical College.

Anatomy, Physiology, Materia Medica, and Therapeutics, Surgery, Midwifery, and Medicine are the chief branches taught. Complete courses of lectures are delivered in the Hindoostanee language on the above subjects. The period of study usually found necessary to qualify a pupil for graduating is from five to seven years. After an examination conduct by a committee of medical officers unconnected with the institution, successful candidates are presented with diplomas by the Minister, and are thus fairly admitted to the ranks of the medical profession. Members of the committee have declared with surprise that some of the graduates were competent to pass the degree tests before the Board of London or Edinburgh.

Students are not required to pay fees. On the contrary, they receive small stipends from His Highness's Government during their period of study.

The school has turned out in all 45 graduates since its first establishment.

The number of students in regular attendance during the past session was 57. Of these, seven received their diplomas at the end of the years, and became eligible for government service.

The Roman Catholic Mission started a school in 1855, which later on developed into the All Saints School in Hyderabad. After Sir Salar Jung became Minister in 1853 he initiated the first educational institution in the State. In 1855 he founded the Darul-ulum or Oriental College at Hyderabad. The languages taught at this institution were English, Arabic, Persian, Telugu, and Marathi. A Board of Governors was appointed and admissions to the school were granted by the Minister personally. A small monthly fee was charged, quarterly examinations were held by the Board of Governors and prizes consisting of books and scholarships varying from Rs. 8 to Rs. 50 per mensem were awarded annually by the Minister.

In reacting to Western influence the name of Shamsul-Umra stands out prominently. He was the premier nobleman of Hyderabad. He was born in 1783 and died in 1863. He was from the very beginning of a scientific bent of mind. He has been described in 1808 A.D. as follow[25]:

Shams-ool-Oomrah, the nominee of the English Government, was at this period about twenty-eight years of age, of a mild disposition and manners, and handsome in person. He was luxurious in all articles of European manufacture, and was ambitious of having his house, furniture, and equipage as nearly as possible conformable to European customs. He took great delight in mechanics, in all manner of handicraft work, and in the popular experiments of natural philosophy. He devoted nearly the whole of his time to these pursuits, leaving the management of his affairs and the command of his party to his maternal uncle, Umjid-ool-Moolk.

Shams-ool-Omra took great interest in the propagation of learning and the production of suitable literature on various subjects especially of a scientific nature. He himself was an author of number of books. Perceiving very early that what the people needed was the acquisition of knowledge through translations of useful works in Indian Languages, he established a Translation Bureau in Hyderabad in 1834 A.D. This Bureau was in existence till 1857 A.D. and a number of works were brought out by this Bureau. The Bureau was established in the Jahan-numa Palace of Shams-ool-Omra. This nobleman had also established a press about the same time. This was known as the *Sangi Chhapekhana* or the stone press. We get a few names of the translators attached to the Translation Bureau. They are:

1. Ghulam Mohiuddin Hyderabadi.
2. Mir Amman Ali Dehlvi.
3. Mr. Jones.
4. Monseigneur Nandres.
5. Mir Shujat Ali Karam.
6. Ratan Lal.
7. Mr. Joseph.

Shams-ool-Omra was very well acquainted with English and French and, as has been noted above, was himself the author of works on science. From the records it appears that about fifty of the works published by the Translation Bureau covered the subjects of theology, mathematics, geometry, physics, chemistry, astronomy, medicine—Western as well as Unani, engineering, history and literature. A majority of them was in Urdu, while a few were in Persian. Shams-ool-Omra and his sons also wrote on scientific subjects. The publication of these works was a great landmark in the history of Hyderabad as for the first time subjects of modern education and thought began to be popularised, particularly in the Indian languages.

Shams-ool-Omra also started a number of schools, the most important of which was located in his palace and served as a centre for higher learning through the medium of Urdu. This school was known as Madras-e-Fakhria and was established in the year 1829. The subjects taught in this school were related not only to theology but to natural sciences like physics, chemistry, astronomy and mathematics. Students from this school were later admitted into the medical school started in the Residency in the year 1844 A.D. The strength of the school in 1854 A.D. was 428.

Besides the school, press and Translation Bureau Shams-ool-Omra maintained in his palace a very good library of books in Urdu, Persian, Arabic, English and French. He subscribed to a number of periodicals and newspapers. Old files of these papers are still available in the library of the Paigah noblemen. Names of some of the periodicals are noted below:

1. Majm-ul-Akhbar (Persian), Bombay, 1843 A.D.
2. Kiran-ul-Saaidin (Urdu), Delhi, files for 1847, 1852, 1853, and 1854 A.D.
3. Fawaid-ul-Nazrin (Urdu), Delhi, files for 1849 and 1852 A.D.
4. Azim-ul-Akhbar (Urdu), Madras, files for 1850 to 1854 A.D.
5. Akhbar-e-Malwa (Urdu), files for 1851 and 1853 A.D.
6. Ahasan-ul-Akhbar (Persian), Bombay, files for 1851 and 1853 A.D.
7. Jam-e-Akhbar (Urdu), files for 1853 A.D.
8. Akhbar-ul-Haqaig (Urdu), Agra, files for 1853 A.D.
9. Umdut-ul-Akhbar (Urdu), Bareli, files for 1853 to 1856 A.D.
10. Amin-ul-Akhbar (Urdu), files for 1856 A.D.
11. Kasf-ul-Akhbar (Urdu), Bombay, files for 1869 A.D.

Shams-ool-Umra was the author of two books, *viz..* (1) Shams-ool-Hindsa, a book on geometry, which was published as early as 1823 A.D. This was translated by Shams-ool-Umra himself from the French work of Monsieur Clarke. A second edition of this work was issued in 1830 A.D. This was in Persian. This book was included in the course for the school Madras-e-Fakhria. (2) The second book written by Shams-ool-Omra was also in Persian on geometry. Shams-ool-Omra's sons were also authors of books dealing with subjects like arithmetic, algebra, mensuration, etc. Under their patronage two important works of history were also published, namely *Tarik-e-Rashid-ud-Din Khani* and *Tarikh-e-Khursheed Jahi.*

It will be seen that Shams-ool-Omra was responsible for initiating interest in higher learning through the starting of schools and the absorption of Western knowledge through translations of works of sciences from English and French into Urdu and Persian. The learning of English was slowly becoming popular by 1858 A.D. Shams-ool-Omra was, as remarked above, acquainted with English and French. Salar Jung I become Prime Minister in 1853 and knew English very well. Some of the noblemen had also started learning English. One example is that of Venkattappa Naik, the Raja of Shorapur, who under the tutelage of Meadows Taylor was given a good grounding in English and other subjects. It is well-known that Raja Venkattappa Naik later took a prominent part in the affairs of 1857 A.D. Thus society in Hyderabad was steadily reacting to Western influences during the first half of the 19th century. The early French influence, the establishment of an English colony in Hyderabad and Secunderabad and the existence of European Officers in the Nizam's army made possible a closer contact between the Europeans and the people of Hyderabad. The results are seen in the starting of Mission Schools like the Saint George's Grammar School, the All Saints School, the establishment of a Medical School under the patronage of the Nizam, the establishment of the Darul-Ulum High School for the teaching of English along with Persian and other subjects and the independent efforts of men like Shams-ool-Omra in the field of education and in the production of scientific literature. There were also anti-English sentiments in Hyderabad which simmered from 1800 A.D. The people in Hyderabad were in touch with the affairs of Northern India, the Maratha States. Western India and Central India. The constant influx of people from Northern India, especially the trans-Indus Rohillas, the Sikhs and leading families of U.P. and Delhi, enabled a close touch to be maintained between Hyderabad and the other parts of the country. Maratha political life also dominated in Hyderabad till at least 1820 A.D. British policy in India. Afghanistan and Burma was followed keenly in Hyderabad. Sir Charles Metcalfe recalls the anxious inquiries, which the *qiladar* of Bidar was making about the fortunes of the British in the Burma campaign during the regime of Lord Amherst.

Raja Chandulal, who was the virtual dictator of Hyderabad from 1808 A.D. to 1843 A.D. was himself a Panjabi and probably induced the influx of a number of Sikhs into the State. He had received a letter from Maharaja Ranjit Singh in 1810 A.D. touching on the general situation in Hyderabad. In fact, General Fraser himself was struck by the intimate knowledge of Sikh polities which Chandulal possessed. The Afghan War was also followed very keenly in Hyderabad by the general public The Wahabi Conspiracy of 1839 show how Hyderabad had become a centre of acute anti-British sentiments.

Thus throughout the first half of the 19th century Hyderabad was steadily reacting to Western influences through an attempt to absorb Western knowledge and also through keeping alive the spirit of resistance to the British. How persistent and powerful was this antagonism to the British will be seen from the great outbreak of the year 1857 A.D. and the part which Hyderabad played in it.

NOTES

1. J. W. Kave. *The Administration of the East India Company*, p. 630, *Ganjam District Manual*, p. 153, *Kistna District Manual*, pp. 346-50, *Nellore District Gazetteer*, pp. 235-236.
2. *Cuddapah District Manual*, p. 110.
3. S. B. Chaudhuri, op. cit., p. 133.
4. *Cuddapah District Manual*, pp. 112-115.
5. *Godavari District Manual*, Chapter XV.
6. *Ibid.*, pp. 78-79.
7. *Cuddapah District Manual*, pp. 104-105.
8. *Bellary District Gazetteer*, pp. 45-50.
9. *Vizagapatam District Gazetteer*, Vol. I, pp. 312-313.
10. *Vizagapatam District Gazetteer*, pp. 287-289.
11. *Ibid.*, p. 304.
12. *Vizagapatam District Gazetteer*, Vol. I, pp. 46-54.
13. *Ibid.*, pp. 317-318.
14. *Cambridge History of India*, Vol. V, p. 281.
15. A.V. Ramana Rao, *The Economic Development of Andhra Pradesh (1766-1957)*, p. 16.

16. *Cambridge History of India*, Vol. V, pp. 467-468.
17. S. B. Chaudhuri, op. cit., p. 151.
18. *Ganjam District Manual*, p. 151.
19. *Ganjam District Manual*, p. 157.
20. *Ibid*.
21. *Ganjam District Manual*, pp. 170-171. S. B. Chaudhuri, *Civil Disturbances during the British Rule in India*, p. 143.
22. *The Cambridge History of India*, Vol. V, p. 463.
23. Aitchison, op. cit., Vol. V, p. 23.
24. *Hyderabad Affairs*, Vol. V, pp. 282-283.
25. *Our Faithful Ally, the Nizam* by Capt. Hastings Fraser, p. 230.

CHAPTER 5

The Counter-Insurgency[1]

I

When a peasant rose in revolt at any time or place under the Raj, he did so necessarily and explicitly in violation of a series of codes which defined his very existence as a member of that colonial, and still largely semi-feudal society. For his subalternity was materialised by the structure of property, institutionalised by law, sanctified by religion and made tolerable—and even desirable—by tradition. To rebel was indeed to destroy man of those familiar signs which he had learned to read and manipulate in order to extract a meaning out of the harsh world around him and live with it. The risk in 'turning things upside down' under these conditions was indeed so great that he could hardly afford to engage in such a project in a state of absent-mindedness.

There is nothing in the primary sources of historical evidence to suggest anything other than this. These give the lie to the myth, retailed so often by careless and impressionistic writing on the subject, of peasant insurrections being purely spontaneous and unpremeditated affairs. The truth is quite to the contrary. It would be difficult to cite and uprising on any significant scale that was not in fact preceded either by less militant types of mobilisation when other means had been tried and found wanting or by parley among its principals seriously to weigh the pros and cons of any recourse to arms. In events so very different from each other in content, character and the composition of participants such as the Rangpur *dhing* against

Debi Sinha (1783), the Barasat *bidroha* led by Titu Mir (1831), the Santal *hool* (1855) and the 'blue mutiny' of 1860 the protagonists in each case had tried out petitions, deputations or other forms of supplication before actually declaring war on their oppressors.[2] Again, the revolts of the Kol (1732), the Santal and the Munda (1899-1900) as well as the Rangpur *dhing* and the jacqueries in Allahabad and Ghazipur districts during the Sepoy Rebellion of 1857-8 (to name only two out of many instances in that remarkable series) had all been inaugurated by planned and in some cases protracted consultation among the representatives of the local peasant masses.[3] Indeed there is hardly an instance of the peasantry, whether the cautious and earthy villagers of the plains or the supposedly more volatile *adivasis* of the upland tracts, stumbling or drifting into rebellion. They had far too much at stake and would not launch into it except as a deliberate, even if desperate, way out of an intolerable condition of existence. Insurgency, in other words, was a motivated and conscious undertaking on the part of the rural masses.

Yet this consciousness seems to have received little notice in the literature on the subject. Historiography has been content to deal with the peasant rebel merely as an empirical person or member of a class, but not as an entity whose will and reason constituted the praxis called rebellion. The omission is indeed dyed into most narratives by metaphors assimilating peasant revolts to natural phenomena: they break out like thunder storms, heave like earthquakes, spread like wildfires, infect like epidemics. In other words, when the proverbial clod of earth turns, this is a matter to be explained in terms of natural history. Even when this historiography is pushed to the point of producing an explanation in rather more human terms it will do so by assuming an identity of nature and culture, a hall-mark, presumably, of a very low state of civilisation and exemplified in 'those periodical outbursts of crime and lawlessness to which all wild tribes are subject', as the first historian of the Chuar rebellion put it.[4]

Alternatively, an explanation will be sought in an enumeration of causes—of, say, factors of economic and political deprivation which do not relate at all to the peasant's consciousness or do so negatively—triggering off rebellion as—a sort of reflex action, that is, as an instinctive and almost mindless response to physical suffering of one kind or another (e.g. hunger, torture, forced labour, etc.) or as a passive reaction to some initiative of his superordinate enemy. Either way insurgency is regarded as *external* to the peasant's consciousness and Cause in made to stand in as a phantom surrogate for Reason, the logic of that consciousness.

II

How did historiography come to acquire this particular blind spot and never find a cure? For an answer one could start by having a close look at its constituting elements and examine those cuts, seams and stitches—those cobbling marks—which tell us about the material it is made of and the manner of its absorption into the fabric of writing.

The corpus of historical writing on peasant insurgency in colonial India is made up of three types of discourse. These may be described as *primary, secondary* and *tertiary* according to the order of their appearance in time and their filiation. Each of these is differentiated from the other two by the degree of its formal and/or acknowledged (as opposed to real and/or tacit) identification with an official point of view, by the measure of its distance from the event to which it refers, and by the ratio of the distributive and integrative components in its narrative.

To begin with primary discourse, it is almost without exception official in character—official in a broad sense of the term. That is, it originated not only with bureaucrats, soldiers, sleuths and others directly employed by the government, but also with those in the non-official sector who were symbiotically related to the Raj, such as planters, missionaries, traders, technicians and so on among the whites and landlords, moneylenders, etc. among the natives. It was official also in so far as it was meant primarily for administrative use—for the information of government, for action on its part and for the determination of its policy. Even when it incorporated statements emanating from 'the other side', from the insurgents or their allies for instance, as it often did by way of direct or indirect reporting in the body of official correspondence or even more characteristically as 'enclosures' to the latter, this was done only as a part of an argument prompted by administrative concern. In other words, whatever its particular form—and there was indeed an amazing variety ranging from the exordial letter, telegram, despatch and communique to the terminal summary, report, judgement and proclamation—its production and circulation were both necessarily contingent on reasons of State.

Yet another of the distinctive features of this type of discourse is its immediacy. This derived from two conditions: first, that statements of this class were written either concurrently with or soon after the event, and secondly, that this was done by the participants concerned, a 'participant' being defined for this purpose in the broad sense of a contemporary involved in the event either in action or indirectly as an onlooker. This would exclude of course that genre of retrospective writing in which, as in some memoirs, an event and its recall are separated by a considerable hiatus, but would still leave a massive documentation—'primary sources' as it is known in the trade—to speak to the historian with a sort of ancestral voice and make him feel close to his subject.

The two specimens quoted below are fairly representative of this type. One of these relates to the Barasat uprising of 1831 and the other to the Santal rebellion of 1855.

TEXT I[5]

To the Deputy Adjutant General of the Army

Sir,

Authentic information having reached government that a body of *Fanatic Insurgents* are now committing *the most daring and wanton atrocities on the Inhabitants* of the Country in the neighbourhood of Tippy in the Magistracy of Barasat and have set at defiance and repulsed the utmost force that the local Civil Authority could assemble for their apprehension, I am directed by the Hon'ble Vice President in Council to request that you will without delay Communicate to the General Officer Commanding the Presidency Division the orders of Government that one Complete Battalion of Native Infantry from Barrackpore and two Six Pounders manned with the necessary compliment (sic) of Golundaze from Dum Dum, the whole under the Command of a Field Officer of judgement and decision, be immediately directed to proceed and rendezvous at Barasat when they will be joined by I Havildar and 12 Troopers of the 3rd Regiment of Light Cavalry now forming the escort of the Hon'ble the Vice President.

2nd. The Magistrate will meet the Officer Commanding the Detachment at Barasat and will afford the necessary information for his guidance relative to the position of the Insurgents; but without having any authority to interfere in such Military operations as the Commanding Officer of the Detachemerts may deem expedient, for the purpose of routing or seizing or in the event of resistance destroying those who persevere in *defying the authority of the State and disturbing the public tranquil[l]ity.*

3rd. It is concluded that the service will not be of such a protracted nature as to require a larger supply of ammunition than may be carried in Pouch and in two Tumbrils for the Guns, and that no difficulties will occur respecting carriage. In the contrary event any aid needed will be furnished.

4th. The Magistrate will be directed to give every assistance regarding supplies and other requisites for the Troops.

Council Chamber — I am & ca

10th November 1831 — (Sd.) Wm. Casement Coll.

Secy. to Govt. Mily. Dept.

TEXT II[6]

From W.C. Taylor Esqre.

To F. S. Mudge Esqre.

Dated 7th July 1855

My dear Mudge,

There is a great gathering of Sonatals 4 or 5000 men at a place about 8 miles off and I understand that they are all well armed with Bows and arrows, Tulwars, Spears & ca. and that *it is their intention to attack all the Europeans round and plunder and murder them. The cause of all this is that one of their Gods is supposed to have taken the Flesh and to have made his appearance at some place near this, and that it is his intention to reign as a King over all this part of India, and has ordered the Sontals to collect and put to death all the Europeans and influential Natives round. As this is the nearest point to the gathering I suppose it will be first attacked* and think it would be best for you to send notice to the authorities at Berhampore and ask for military aid as *it is not at all a nice look out being murdered* and as far as I can make out this is a *rather serious affair.*

Sreecond Yours & ca

7th July 1855 /Signed/ W. C. Taylor

Nothing could be more immediate than these texts. Written as soon as these events were acknowledged as rebellion by those who had the most to fear from it, they are among the very first records we have on them in the collections of the India Office Library and the West Bengal State Archives. As the evidence on the 1831 *bidroha* shows[7] it was not until 10 November that the Calcutta authorities came to recognise the violence reported from the Barasat region for what it was—a full-blooded insurrection led by Titu Mir and his men. Colonel Casement's letter identifies for us that moment when the hitherto unknown leader of a local peasantry entered the lists against the Raj and thereby made his way into history. The date of the other document too commemorates a beginning—that of the Santal *hool*. It was on that very day, 7 July 1855, that the assassination of Mahesh *daroga* following an encounter between his police and peasants gathered at Bhagnadihi detonated the uprising. The report was loud enough to register in that note scribbled in obvious alarm at Sreecond by an European employee of the East India Railway for the benefit of his colleague and the *sarkar*. Again, these are words that convey as directly as possible the impact of a peasant revolt on its enemies in its first sanguinary hours.

III

None of this instantaneousness percolates through to the next level—that of the secondary discourse. The latter draws on primary discourse as *material* but transforms it at the same time.

To contrast the two types one could think the first as historiography in a raw, primordial state or as an embryo yet to be articulated into an organism with discrete limbs, and the second as the processed product, however crude the processing, a duly constituted if infant discourse.

The difference is quite obviously a function of time. In the chronology of this particular corpus the secondary follows the primary at a distance and opens up a perspective to turn an event into history in the perception not only of those outside it but of the participants as well. It was thus that Mark Thornhill, Magistrate of Mathura during he summer of 1857 when a mutiny of the Treasury Guard sparked off jacqueries all over the district, was to reflect on the altered status of his own narrative in which he figured as a protagonist himself. Introducing his well-known memoirs, *The Personal Adventures and Experiences Of A Magistrate During The Rise, Progress, And Suppression Of The Indian Mutiny* (London, 1884) twenty-seven years after the event he wrote:

> After the suppression of the Indian Mutiny, I commenced to write an account of my adventures . . . by the time my narrative was completed, the then interest of the public in the subject was exhausted. Years have since passed, and an interest of another kind has arisen. The events of that time have become history, and to that history my story may prove a contribution . . . I have therefore resolved to publish my narrative. . .

Shorn of contemporaneity a discourse is thus recovered as an element of the past and classified as history. This change, aspectual as well as categorial, sites it at the very intersection of colonialism and historiograpy, endowing it with a duplex character linked at the same time to a system of power and the particular manner of its representation.

Its authorship is in itself witness to this intersection and Thornhill was by no means the only administrator turned historian. He was indeed one of many officials, civilian and military, who wrote retrospectively on popular disturbances in rural India under the Raj. Their statements, taken together, fall into two classes. First, there were those which were based on the writers' own experience as participants. Memoirs of one kind or another these were written either at a considerable delay after the events narrated or almost concurrently with them but intended, unlike primary discourse, for a public readership. The latter, an important distinction, shows how the colonialist mind managed to serve Clio and counter-insurgency at the same time so that the presumed neutrality of one could have hardly been left unaffected by the passion of the other, a point to which we shall soon return. Reminiscences of both kinds abound in the literature on the Mutiny, which dealt with the violence of the peasantry (especially in the North Western Provinces and Central India) no less than with that of the sepoys. Accounts such as Thornhill's written long after the event, were matched by near contemporary ones such as Dunlop's *Service and Adventure with Khakee Ressallah; or Meerut Volunteer Horse during the Mutinies of 1857-58* (London, 1858) and Edwards' *Personal Adventures during the Indian Rebellion in Rohilcund, Futtehghur, and Oudh* (London, 1858) to mention only two out of a vast outcrop intended to cater for a public who could not have enough of tales of horror and glory.

The other class of writings to qualify as secondary discourse is also the work of administrators. They too addressed themselves to a predominantly non-official readership but on themes not directly related to their own experience. Their work includes some of the most widely used and highly esteemed accounts of peasant uprisings written either as monographs on particular events, such as Jamini Mohan Ghosh's on the Sannyasi-and-Faqir disturbances and J.C. Price's on the Chuar Rebellion, or as statements included in more comprehensive histories like W. W. Hunter's story of the Santal *hool in The Annals of Rural Bengal.* Apart from these there were those distinguished contributions made by some of the best minds in the Civil Service to the historical chapters of the *District Gazetteers.* Altogether they constitute a substantial body of writing which enjoys much authority with all students of the subject and there is hardly any historiography at the next, that is, tertiary level of discourse that does not rely on these for sustenance.

The prestige of this genre is to no mean extent due to the

aura of impartiality it has about it. By keeping their narrative firmly beyond the pale of personal involvement these authors managed, if only by implication, to confer on it a semblance of truth. As officials they were carriers of the will of the state no doubt. But since they wrote about a past in which they did not figure as functionaries themselves, their statements are taken to be more authentic and less biased than those of their opposite numbers whose accounts, based on reminiscences, were necessarily contaminated by their intervention in rural disturbances as agents of the Raj. By contrast the former are believed to have approached the narrated events from the outside. As observers separated clinically from the site and subject of diagnosis they are supposed to have found for their discourse a niche in that realm of perfect neutrality—the realm of History—over which the Aorist and the Third Person preside.

IV

How valid is this claim to neutrality? For an answer we may not take any bias for granted in this class of historical work from the mere fact of its origin with authors committed to colonialism. To take that as self-evident would be to deny historiography the possibility of acknowledging its own inadequacies and thus defeat the purpose of the present exercise. As should be clear from what follows, it is precisely by refusing to *prove* what appears as obvious that historians of peasant insurgency remain trapped—in the obvious. Criticism must therefore start not by naming bias but by examining the components of the discourse, vehicle of all ideology, for the manner in which these might have combined to described any particular figure of the past.

The components of both types of discourse and their varieties discussed so far are what we shall call segments. Made up of the same linguistic material, that is strings of words of varying lengths, they are of two kinds which may be designated, according to their function, as indicative and interpretative. A gross differentiation, this is meant to assign to them, within a given text, the role respectively of reporting and explaining. This however does not imply their mutual segregation. On the contrary they are often found embedded in each other not merely as a matter of fact but of necessity.

One can see in Texts 1 and 2 how such imbrication works. In both of them the straight print stands for the indicative segments and the italics for the interpretative. Laid out according to no particular pattern in either of these letters they interpenetrate and sustain each other in order to give the documents their meaning and in the process endow some of the strings with an ambiguity that is inevitably lost in this particular manner of typographical representation. However, the rough outline of a division of functions between the two classes emerges even from this schema—the indicative stating (that is reporting) the actual and anticipated actions of the rebels and their enemies, and the interpretative commenting them in order to understand (that is to explain) their significance.

The difference between them corresponds to that between the two basic components of any historical discourse which, following Roland Barthes' terminology, we shall call *functions* and *indices*.[2] The former are segments that make up the linear sequence of a narrative. Contiguous, they operate in a relation of solidarity in the sense of mutually implying each other and add up to increasingly larger strings which combine to produce the aggregative statement. The latter may thus be regarded as a sum of micro-sequences to each of which, however important or otherwise, it should be possible to assign names by a metalinguistic operation using terms that may or may not belong to the text under consideration. It is thus that the functions of a folk-tale have been named by Bremond, after Propp, as *Fraud, Betrayal, Struggle, Contract,* etc. and those of a triviality such as the offer of a cigarette in a James Bond story designated by Barthes as *offering, accepting, lighting,* and *smoking*. One may perhaps take a cue from this procedure to define a historical statement as a discourse with a name subsuming again number of named sequences. Hence it should be possible to speak of a hypothetical narrative called 'The Insurrection of Titu Mir' made up of a number of sequences in clouding Text I quoted above.

Let us give this document a name and call it, say, *Calcutta Council Acts.* (Alternatives such as *Outbreak of Violence or Army*

Called Up should also do and be analysable in terms corresponding to, though not identical with, those which follow.) In broad terms the message *Calcutta Council Acts* (C) in our text can be read as a combination of two groups of sequences called *alarm* (a) and *intervention* (b), each of which is made up of a pair of segments—the former of *insurrection breaks out* (a′) and *information received* (a″) and the latter of *decision to call up army* (b′) and *order issued* (b″), one of the constituents in each pair being represented in its turn by yet another linked series—(a′) by *atrocities committed* (a_1) and *authority defied* (a_2) and (b″) by *infantry to proceed* (b_1), *artillery to support* (b_2) and *magistrate to co-operate* (b_3). In other words the narrative in this document can be written up in three equivalent steps so that,

$$
\begin{aligned}
C &\equiv (a+b) && \text{I} \\
&\equiv (a' + a'') + (b' + b'') && \text{II} \\
&\equiv (a_1 + a_2) + a'' + b' + (b_1 + b_2 + b_3) && \text{III}
\end{aligned}
$$

It should be clear from this arrangement that not all the elements of step II can be expressed in micro-sequences of the same order. Hence we are left at step III with a concatenation in which segments drawn from different levels of the discourse are imbricated to constitute a roughly hewn and uneven structure. In so far as functional units of the lowest denomination like these are what a narrative has as its syntagmatic relata its course can never be smooth. The hiatus between the loosely cobbled segments is necessarily charged with uncertainty, with 'moments of risk' and every micro-sequence terminates by opening up alternative possibilities only one of which is picked up by the next sequence as it carries on with the story. 'Du Pont, Bond's future partner, offers him a light from his lighter but Bond refuses; the meaning of this bifurcation is that Bond instinctively fears a booby-trapped gadget.'[9] What Barthes identifies thus as 'bifurcation' in fiction, has its parallels in historical discourse as well. The alleged commitment of atrocities (a_1) in that official despatch of 1831 cancels out the belief in the peaceful propagation of Titu's new doctrine which had already been known to the authorities but ignored so far as inconsequential. The expression, *authority defied* (a_2), which refers to the rebels having 'set at defiance and repulsed the utmost force that the local Civil Authority could assemble for their apprehension', has as its other if unseated term his efforts to persuade the government by petition and deputation to offer redress for the grievances of his co-regionalists. And so on. Each of these elementary functional units thus implies a node which has not quite materialised into an actual development, a sort of zero sign by means of which the narrative affirms its tension. And precisely because history as the verbal representation by man of his own past is by its very nature so full of hazard, so replete indeed with the verisimilitude of sharply differentiated choices, that it never ceases to excite. The historical discourse is the world's oldest thriller.

V

Sequential analysis thus shows a narrative to be a concatenation of not so closely aligned functional units. The latter are dissociative in their operation and emphasise the analytic rather than the synthetic aspect of a discourse. As such they are not what, by themselves, generate its meaning. Just as the sense of a word (e.g. 'man') is not fractionally represented in each of the letters (e.g. M, A, N) which make up its graphic image nor of a phrase (e.g. 'once upon a time') in its constituting words taken separately, so also the individual segments of a discourse cannot on their own tell us what it signifies. Meaning in each instance is the work of a process of integration which complements that of sequential articulation. As Benveniste has put it, in any language 'it is dissociation which divulges to us its formal constitution and integration its signifying units.'[10]

This is true of the language of history as well. The integrative operation is carried out in its discourse by the other class of basic narrative units, that is, *indices*. A necessary and indispensable correlate of *functions* they are distinguished from the latter in some important respects:

> Indices, because of the vertical nature of their relations are truly semantic units: unlike 'functions' . . . they refer to a signified, not to an 'operation'. The ratification of indices is 'higher up' . . . a paradigmatic ratification. That of functions, by contrast, is always 'further on', is a

syntagmatic ratification. *Functions* and *indices* thus overlay another classic distinction: functions involve metonymic relata, indices metaphoric relata; the former correspond to a functionality of doing, the latter to a functionality of being.[11]

The vertical intervention of indices in a discourse is possible because of the disruption of its linearity by a process corresponding to dystaxia in the behaviour of many natural languages. Bally who has studied this phenomenon in much detail finds that one of several conditions of its occurrence in French is 'when parts of the same sign are separated' so that the expression, 'elle a pardonné' taken in the negative, is splintered and re-assembled as 'elle *ne nous a jamais plus pardonné*.'[12] Similarly the simple predictive in Bengali shé jābé' can be re-written by the insertion of an interrogative or a string of negative conditionals between the two words to produce respectively 'shé ki jābé' and 'shé *nā hoy nā jābé*'.

In a historical narrative too it is a process of 'distension and expansion' of its syntagm which helps paradigmatic elements to infiltrate and reconstitute its discrete segments into a meaningful whole. It is precisely thus that the co-ordination of the metonymic and metaphorical axes is brought about in a statement and the necessary interaction of its functions and indices actualised. However these units are not distributed in equal proportions in all texts: some have a greater incidence of one kind than of the other. As a result a discourse could be either predominantly metonymic or metaphorical depending on whether as significantly larger number of its components are syntagmatically ratified or paradigmatically.[13] Our Text I is of the first type. One can see the formidable and apparently impenetrable array of its metonymic relata in step III of the sequential analysis given above. Here at last we have the perfect authentication of the idiot's view of history as one damn'd thing after another: *rising-information-decision-order*. However, a closer look at the text can detect chinks which have allowed 'comment,' to worm its way through the plate armour of 'fact'. The italicized expressions are witness to this paradigmatic intervention and indeed its measure. Indices, they play the role of *adjectives or epithets* as opposed to verbs which, to speak in terms of homology between sentence and narrative, is the role of functions.[14] Working intimately together with the latter they make the despatch into more than a mere register of happenings and help to inscribe into it a meaning, an interpretation so that the protagonists emerge from it not as peasants but as *'Insurgents'*, not as Musalman but as *'fanatic'*; their action not as resistance to the tyranny of the rural elite but as *'the most daring and wanton atrocities on the inhabitants'*; their project not as a revolt against zamindari but as *'defying the authority of the State'*, not as a search for an alternative order in which the peace of the countryside would not be violated by the officially condoned anarchy of semi-feudal landlordism but as, *'disturbing the public tranquil[l]ity.'*

If the intervention of indices 'substitutes meaning for the straight-forward copy of the events recounted,[15] in a text so charged with metonymy as the one discussed above, it may be trusted to do so to an even greater degree in discourses which are predominantly metaphorical. This should be evident from Text 2 where the element of comment, italicized by us, largely out-weighs that of report. If the latter is represented as a concatenation of three functional sequences, namely, *armed Santals gathering, authorities to be alerted and military aid requested,* it can be seen how the first of these has been separated from the rest by the insertion of a large chunk of explanatory material and how the others too are enveloped and sealed off by comment. The latter is inspired by the fear that Sreecond being *'the nearest point to the gathering . . . will be first attacked'* and of course *'it is not at all a nice look out being murdered'*. Notice, however, that this fear justifies itself politically, that is, by imputing to the Santals an *'intention to attack . . . plunder . . . and put to death all the Europeans and influential Natives'* so that *'one of their Gods'* in human form may *'reign as a King over all this part of India.'* Thus, this document is neutral in its attitude to the events witnessed and put up as 'evidence' before the court of history it can hardly be expected to testify with impartiality. On the contrary it is the voice of committed colonialism. It has already made a choice between the prospect of Santal self-rule in Damin-i-Koh and the continuation of the British Raj and identifies what is allegedly good for the promotion of one as fearsome and catastrophic for the other—as *'a rather serious affair.'* In other words the indices in this discourse—as well as in the one discussed above—introduce us to a particular code so constituted that for each of its signs we have an antonym, a counter-message, in another code. To borrow a binary representation made famous by Mao Tse-tung,[16] the reading, *'Its terrible!'* for any element in one must show up in the other as *'It's fine!'* for a corresponding element and vice versa. To put this clash of codes graphically one can arrange the indices italicized below of Texts 1 and 2 in a matrix called 'Terrible' (in conformity to the adjectival attribute of units of this class) in such a way as to indicate their mapping into the implied, though unstated terms (given in straight types) of a corresponding matrix 'Fine.'

TERRIBLE	*FINE*
Insurgents	peasants
fanatic	Islamic puritan
daring and wanton atrocities on the Inhabitants	resistance to oppression
defying the authority of the State	revolt against zamindari
disturbing the public tranquil (l) ity	struggle for a better order
intention to attack, etc.	intention to punish oppressors
one of their Gods to reign as a King	Santal self-rule

What comes out of the interplay of these mutually implied but opposed matrices is that our texts are not the record of observations uncontaminated by bias, judgement and opinion. On the contrary, they speak of a total complicity. For if the expressions in the right-hand column taken together may be said to stand for insurgency, the code which contains all signifies of the subaltern practice of 'turning things upside down' and the consciousness that informs it, then the other column must stand for its opposite, that is, counter-insurgency. The antagonism between the two is irreducible and there in nothing in this to leave room for neutrality. Hence these documents make no sense except in terms of a code of pacification which, under the Raj, was a complex of coercive intervention by the State and its protégés, the native elite, with arms and words. Representatives of the primary type of discourse in the historiography of peasant revolts, these are specimens of the prose of counter-insurgency.

VI

How far does secondary discourse too share such commitment? Is it possible for it to speak any other prose than that of a counter-insurgency? Those narratives of this category in which their authors figure among the protagonists are of course suspect almost by definition, and the presence of the grammatical first person in these must be acknowledged as a sign of complicity. The question however is whether the loss of objectivity on this account is adequately made up by the consistent use of the aorist in such writings. For as Benveniste observes, the historical utterance admits of three variations of the past tense—that is, the aorist, the imperfect and the pluperfect, and of course the present is altogether excluded.[17] This condition is indeed satisfied by reminiscences separated by a long enough hiatus from the events concerned. What has to be found out therefore is the extent to which the force of the preterite corrects the bias caused by the absence of the third person.

Mark Thornhill's memoirs of the Mutiny provide us with a text in which the author looks back at a series of events he had experienced twenty-seven years ago. 'The events of that time' has 'turned into history', and he intends, as he says in the extract quoted above, to make a contribution 'to that history', and thus produce what we have defined as a particular kind of secondary discourse. The difference inscribed in it by that interval is perhaps best grasped by comparing it with some samples of primary discourse we have on the same subject from the same author. Two of these[18] may be read together as a record of his perception of what happened at the Mathura Sadar Station and the surrounding countryside between 14 May and 3 June 1857. Written by him donning the district magistrate's topee and addressed to his superiors—one on 5 June 1857, that is, within forty-eight hours of the terminal date of the period under discussion, and the other on 10 August 1858 when the events were still within vivid recall as a very recent past—these letters coincide in scope with that of the narrative covering the same three weeks in the first ninety pages of his book written nearly three decades later donning the historian's hat.

The letters are both predominantly metonymic in character. Originating as they did almost from within the related experience itself they are necessarily foreshortened and tell the reader in breathless sequences about some of the happenings of that extraordinary summer. The syntagm thus takes on a semblance of factuality with hardly any room in it for comment. Yet here again the welding of the functional units can be seen, on close inspection, to be less solid than at first sight. Embedded in them there are indices revealing the anxieties of the local custodian of law and order ('the state of the district generally is such as to *defy all control*'; '*the law* is at a *standstill*'), his fears ('*very alarming* rumours of the approach of the rebel army'), his moral disapprobation of the activities of the armed villagers ('the disturbances in the district . . . increasing . . . in . . . *enormity*'), his appreciation by contrast of the native collaborators hostile to the insurgents (' . . . 'the Seths' house . . . *received us most kindly*'). Indices such as these are ideological birth marks displayed prominently on much of this type of material relating to peasant revolts. Indeed, taken together with some other relevant textual features—e.g. the abrupt mode of address in these documents so revealing of the shock and terror generated by the *émeute*—they accuse all such allegedly 'objective' evidence on the militancy of the rural masses to have been tainted at its source by the prejudice and partisan outlook of their enemies. If historicans fail to take notice of these tell-tale signs branded on the staple of their trade, that is a fact which must be explained in terms of the optics of a colonialist historiography rather than constructed in favour of the presumed objectivity of their 'primary sources'.

There is nothing immediate or abrupt about the corresponding secondary discourse. On the contrary it has various perspectives built into it to give it a depth in time and following from this temporal determination, its meaning. Compare for instance the narration of events in the two versions for any particular day—for, say, 14 May 1857 at the very beginning of our three-week period. Written up in a very short paragraph of fifty-seven words in Thornhill's letter of 10 August 1858 this can be represented fully in four pithy segments without any significant loss of message: *mutineers approaching;*

information received from Gurgaon; confirmed by Europeans north of the district; women and non-combattants sent off to Agra. Since the account starts, for all practical purposes, with this entry, there are no exordia to serve as its context, giving this instant take-off the sense, as we have noticed, of a total surprise. In the book however that same instant is provided with a background spread over four and a half months and three pages (pp. 1-3). All of this time and space is devoted to some carefully chosen details of the author's life and experience in the period preceding the Mutiny. These are truly *significant*. As indices they prepare the reader for what is to come and help him to *understand* the happenings of 14 May and after, when these enter into the narrative at staggered stages. Thus the mysterious circulation of *chapatis* in January and the silent but expressive concern on the narrators' brother, a high official over a telegram received at Agra on 12 May conveying the still unconfirmed news of the Meerut uprising, portend the developments two days later at his own district headquarters. Again the trivia about his 'large income and great authority', his house, horses, servants, 'a chest full of silver plate, which stood in the hall and . . . a great store of Cashmere shawls, pearls, and diamonds' all help to index, by contrast, the holocaust which was soon to reduce his authority to nothing, and turn his servants into rebels, his house into a shambles, his property into booty for the plundering poor of town and country. By anticipating the narrated events thus, if only by implication, secondary discourse destroys the entropy of the first, its raw material. Henceforth there will be nothing in the story that can be said to be altogether unexpected.

This effect is the work of the so-called 'organisation shifters'[19] which help the author to superimpose a temporality of his own on that of his theme , that is 'to "dechronologize" the historical thread and restore, if only by way of reminiscence or nostalgia, a Time at once complex, parametric, and non-linear . . . . braiding the chronology of the subject-matter with that of the language-act which reports it.' In the present instance the 'braiding' consists not only in fitting an evocative context to the bare sequence related in that short paragraph of his letter. The shifters disrupt the syntagm twice to insert in the breach, on both occasions, a moment of authorial time suspended between the two poles of 'waiting', a figure ideally constituted to allow the play of digressions, asides and parentheses forming loops and zigzags in a story-line and adding thereby to its depth. Thus, waiting for news about the movements of the mutineers he reflects on the peace of the early evening at the Sadar Station and strays from his account to tell us in violation of the historiographical canon of tense and person: 'The scene was simple and full of the repose of Eastern life. In the times that followed it often recurred to my memory.' And, again, waiting later on for transport to take away the evacuees gathered in his drawing room, he withdraws from that particular night for the education of a few words to comment: 'It was a beautiful room, brightly lighted, gay with flowers. It was the last time I thus saw it, and so it remains impressed on my memory.'

How far does the operation of these shifters help to correct the bias resulting from the writer's intervention in the first person? Not much by this showing. For each of the indices wedged into the narrative represents a principled choice between the terms of a paradigmatic opposition. Between the authority of the head of the district and its defiance by the armed masses, between the habitual servility of his menials and their assertion of self-respect as rebels, between the insignia of his wealth and power (e.g. gold, horses, shawls, bungalow) and their appropriation or destruction by the subaltern crowds, the author, hardly differentiated from the administrator that he was twenty-seven years ago, consistently chooses the former. Nostalgia makes the choice all the more eloquent—a recall of what is thought to be 'fine' such as a peaceful evening or an elegant room emphasising by contrast the 'terrible' aspects of popular violence directed against the Raj. Quite clearly there is a logic to this preference. It affirms itself by negating as series of inversions which, combined with other signs of the same order, constitute a code of insurgency. The pattern of the historian's choice, identical with the magistrate's, conforms thus to a counter-code, the code of counter-insurgency.

VII

If the neutralising effect of the aorist fails thus to prevail over the subjectivity of the protagonist as narrator in this particular genre of secondary discourse, how does the balance of tense and person stand in the other kind of writing within the same category? One can see two distinct idioms at work here, both identified with the standpoint of colonialism but unlike each other in expressing it. The cruder variety is well exemplified in *The Chuar Rebellion of 1799* by J. C. Price. Written long after the events, in 1874, it was obviously meant by the author, Settlement Officer of Midnapur at the time, to serve as a straightforward historical account with no particular administrative end in view. He addressed it to 'the casual reader' as well as to any future Collector of Midnapore', hoping to share with both 'that keen interest which I have felt as I have read the old Midnapore records.'[20] But the author's delight. . . experienced in pouring over these papers' seems to have produced a text almost indistinguishable from the primary discourse used as its source. The latter is, for one thing, conspicuous by its sheer physical presence. Over a fifth of that half of the book which deals specifically with the events of 1799 is made up of direct quotations from those records and another large part of barely modified extracts. More important for us, however, is the evidence we have of the author's identification of his own sentiments with those of that small group of whites who were reaping the whirlwind produced by the wind of a violently disruptive change the Company's governments had sown in the South-Western corner of Bengal. Only the fear of the beleaguered officials at Midnapur station in 1799 turns seventy-five years later into that genocidal hatred characteristic of a genre of post-Mutiny British writing. 'The disinclination of the authorities, civil or military, to proceed in person to help to quell the disturbances is most striking', he writes shaming his compatriots and then goes on to brag:

> In these days of breech-loaders half a dozen Europeans would have been a match for twenty times their number of Chuars. Of course with the imperfect nature of the weapons of that day it could not be expected that Europeans would fruitlessly rush into danger, but I should have expected that the European officers of the station would have in some instances at least courted and met an attack in person and repulsed their assailants. I wonder that no one European officer, civilian or military, with the exception of perhaps

Lieutenant Gill, owned to that sensation of joyous excitement most young men feel now-a-days in field sports, or in any pursuit where there is an element of danger. I think most of us, had we lived in 1799, would have counted it better sport had we bagged a marauding Chuar reeking with blood and spoils, than the largest bear that the Midnapore jungles can produce.[21]

Quite clearly the author's separation from his subject-matter and the difference between the time of the event and that of its narration here have done little to inspire objectivity in him. His passion is apparently of the same order as that of the British soldier who wrote on the eve of the sack of Delhi in 1857: 'I most sincerely trust that the order given when we attack Delhi will be . . . "Kill every one; no quarter is to be given".[22] The historian's attitude to rebels is in this instance indistinguishable from that of the State—the attitude of the hunter to his quarry. Regarded thus an insurgent is not a subject of understanding or interpretation but of extermination, and the discourse of history, far from being neutral, serves directly to instigate official violence.

There were however other writers working within the same genre who are known to have expressed themselves in a less sanguinary idiom. They are perhaps best represented by W. W. Hunter and his account of the Santal insurrection of 1855 in *The Annals of Rural Bengal*. It is, in many respects, a remarkable text. Written within a decade of the Mutiny and twelve years of the *hool*,[23] it has none of that revanchist and racist overtone common to a good deal of Anglo-Indian literature of the period. Indeed the author treats the enemies of the Raj not only with consideration but with respect although they had wiped it off from three Eastern districts in a matter of weeks and held out for five months against the combined power of the colonial army and its newly acquired auxiliaries—railways and the 'electric telegraph.' One of the first modern exercises in the historiography of Indian peasant revolts, it situates the uprising in a cultural and socio-economic context, analyses its causes, and draws on local records and contemporary accounts for evidence about its progress and eventual suppression. Here, to all appearances, we have that classic instance of the author's own bias and opinion dissolving under the operation of the past tense and the grammatical third person. Here, perhaps, historical discourse his come to its own and realised that ideal of an 'apersonal . . . mode of narrative . . . designed to wipe out the presence of the speaker'?[24]

This semblance of objectivity, of the want of any obviously demonstrable bias, has however nothing to do with 'facts speaking for themselves' in a state of pure metonymy unsullied by comment. On the contrary the text is packed with comment. One has to compare it with something like the near contemporary article on this subject in *Calcutta Review* (1856) or even K.K. Datta's history of the *hool* written long after its suppression to realise how little there is in it of the details of what actually happened.[25] Indeed the narration of the event occupies in the book only about 7 per cent of the chapter which builds up climatically towards it, and somewhat less than 50 per cent of the print devoted specifically to this topic within that chapter. The syntagm is broken up again and again by dystaxia and interpretation filters through to assemble the segments into a meaningful whole of a primarily metaphorical character. The consequence of this operation that is most relevant for our purpose here is the way in which it distributes the paradigmatic relata along an axis of historical continuity between a 'before' and an 'after', forelengthening it with a context and extending it into a perspective. The representation of insurgency ends up thus by having its moment intercalated between its past and future so that the particular values of one and the other are rubbed into the event to give it the meaning specific to it.

VIII

To turn first to the context, two-thirds of the chapter which culminates in the history of the insurrection is taken up with an inaugural account of what may be called the natural history of its protagonists. An essay in ethnography this deals with the physical traits, language, traditions, myths, religion, rituals, habitat, environment, hunting and agricultural practices, social organisation and communal government of the Santals of the Birbhum region. There are many details here which index the coming conflict as one of contraries, as between the noble savage of the hills and mean exploiters from the plains—references to his personal dignity ('He does not abase himself to the ground like the rural Hindu'; the Santal woman is 'ignorant of the shrinking squeamishness of the Hindu female', etc.) implying the contrast his would-be reduction to servitude by Hindu moneylenders, his honesty ('Unlike the Hindu, he never thinks of making money by a stranger, scrupulously avoids all topics of business, and feels pained if payment is pressed up him for the milk and fruit which his wife brings out'), the greed and fraud of the alien traders and landlords leading eventually to the insurrection, his aloofness ('The Santals live as much apart as possible from the Hindus'), the *diku's* intrusion into his life and territory and the holocaust which inevitably followed.

These indices given the uprising not only a moral dimension and the values of a just war, but also a depth in time. The latter is realised by the operation of diachronic markers in the text—an imaginary past by creation myths (appropriate for an enterprise taken up on the Thakur's advice) and a real but remote past (befitting a revolt steeped in tradition) by the sherds of prehistory in ritual and speech with the Santals' ceremony of 'Purifying for the Dead' mentioned, for instance, as the trace of 'a faint remembrance of the far-off time when they dwelt beside great rivers' and their language as 'that intangible record on which a nation's past is graven more deeply than on brass tablets or rock inscriptions'.

Moving closer to the event the author provides it with a recent past covering roughly a period of sixty years of 'direct administration' in the area. The moral and temporal aspects of the narrative merge here in the figure of an irreconcilable contradiction. On the one hand there were, according to Hunter, a series of beneficial measures introduced by the government—the Decennial Settlement helping to expand the area under cultivation and induce the Santals, since 1792, to hire themselves out as agricultural labourers; the setting up, in 1832, of an enclosure ringed off by masonry pillars wheel they could colonize virgin land and jungle without fear of harassment from hostile tribes; the development of 'English enterprise' in Bengal in the form of indigo factories for which 'the Santal immigrants afforded a population of day-labourers'; and last but not the least of bonanzas, their absorption by thousands into labour gangs for the construction or railways across that region in 1854. But there were, on the other hand, two sets of factors which combined to undo all the good resulting from colonial rule, namely, the exploitation and oppression of the Santals by greedy and fraudulent Hindu landlords, moneylenders and traders, and the failure of the local administration, its police and the courts to protect them or redress the wrongs they suffered.

IX

This emphasis on contradiction serves on obviously interpretative purpose for the author. It makes it possible for him to locate the cause of the uprising in a failure of the Raj to make its ameliorative aspects prevail over the still lingering defects and shortcomings in its exercise of authority. The account of the event therefore fits directly into the objective stated at the beginning of the chapter, that is, to interest not only the scholar 'in these lapsed races' but the statesman as well. 'The Indian statesman will discover', he had written there referring euphemistically to the makers of British policy in India, 'that these Children of the Forest are . . . amenable to the same reclaiming influences as other men, and that upon their capacity for civilisation the future extension of English enterprise in Bengal in a large measure depends.' It is this concern for 'reclamation' (shorthand for accelerating the transformation of the tribal peasantry into wage labour and harnessing them to characteristically colonialist projects for the exploitation of Indian resources) which explains the mixture of firmness and 'understanding' in Hunter's attitude to the rebellion. A liberal-imperialist he regarded it both as a menace to the stability of the Raj and as a useful critique of its far from perfect administration. So while he censured the government of the day for not declaring Martial Law soon enough in order to cut down the hool at its inception, he was careful to differentiate himself from those of his compatriots who wanted to punish the entire Santal community for the crime of. its rebels and deport overseas the population of the districts involved. A genuinely far-sighted imperialist he looked forward to the day when the tribe, like many other aboriginal peoples of the subcontinent, would demonstrate its capacity for civilisation by acting as in inexhaustible source of cheap labour power.

This vision is inscribed into the perspective with which the narration ends. Blaming the outbreak of the *hool* squarely on that 'cheap and practical administration' which paid no heed to the Santals' complaints and concentrated on tax collection alone it goes on to catalogue the somewhat illusory benefits of 'the more exact system that was introduced after the revolt' to keep the power of the usurers over debtors within the limits of the law, check the use of false weights and measures in retail trade, and ensure the right of bonded labourers to choose freedom by desertion or change of employers. But more than administrative reform it was 'English enterprise' again which radically contributed to the welfare of the tribe. The railways 'completely changed the relation of labour to capital' and did away with that 'natural reason for slavery—to wit, the absence of a wage-fund for free workmen'. The demand for plantation labour in the Assam tea-districts 'was destined still further to improve the position of the Santals' and so was the stimulus for indenturing coolies for the Mauritius and the Carribeans. It was thus that the tribal peasant prospered thanks to the development of a vast sub-continental and overseas labour market within the British Empire. In the Assam tea gardens 'his whole family gets employment, and every additional child, instead of being the means of increasing his poverty, becomes a source of wealth', while the coolies return from Africa or the West Indies 'at the expiry of their contracts with savings averaging £ 20 sterling, a sum sufficient to set up a Santal as a considerable proprietor in his own village.'

Many of these so-called improvements were, as we know now looking back at them across a century, the result of sheer wishful thinking or so ephemeral as not to have mattered at all. The connection between usury and bonded labour continued all through British rule well into independent India. The freedom of the labour market was seriously restricted by the want of competition between British and indigenous capital. The employment of tribal families on tea plantations became a source of cynical exploitation of the labour of women and children. The advantages of mobility and contractually were cancelled out by irregularities in the process of recruitment and the manipulation of the contrary factors of economic dependence and social differentiation by *arkatis*. The system of indenturing helped rather less to liberate servile labour than to develop a sort of second serfdom, and so on.

Yet this vision which never materialised offers an insight into the character of this type of discourse. The perspective it inspired amounted in effect to a testament of faith in colonialism. The *hool* was assimilated there to the career of the Raj and the militant enterprise of a tribal peasantry to free themselves from the triple yoke of *sarkar*, *sahukari* and *zamindari* to 'English enterprise'—the infrastructure of Empire. Hence the objective stated at the beginning of the account could be reiterated towards the end with the author saying that he had written at least 'partly for the instruction which their [the Santals'] recent history furnishes as to the proper method of dealing with the aboriginal races'. The suppression of local peasant revolts was a part of this method, but it was incorporated now in a broader strategy designed to tackle the economic problems of the British Government in India as an element of the global problems of imperial politics. 'These are the problems', says Hunter in concluding the chapter, 'which Indian statesmen during the next fifty years will be called upon to solve. Their predecessors have given civilisation to India; it will be their duty to render that civilisation at once beneficial to the natives and safe for ourselves'. In other words this historiography was assigned a role in a political process that would ensure the security of the Raj by a combination of force to crush rebellion when it occurred and reform to pre-empt it by wrenching the tribal peasantry out of their rural bases and distributing them as cheap labour power for British capital to exploit in India and abroad. The overtly aggressive and nervous prose of counter-insurgency born of the worries of the early colonial days came thus to adopt in this genre of historical writing the firm but benign, authoritarian but understanding idiom of a mature and self-assured imperialism.

X

How is it that even the more liberal type of secondary discourse is unable thus to extricate itself from the code of counter-insurgency? With all the advantage he has of writing in the third person and addressing a distinct past the official turned historian is still far from being impartial where official interests are concerned. His sympathies for the peasants' sufferings and his understanding of what goaded them to revolt, do not, when the crunch comes, prevent him from siding with law and order and justifying the transfer of the campaign against the *hool* from civilian to military hands in order to crush it completely and quickly. And as discussed above, his partisanship over the outcome of the rebellion is matched by his commitment to the aims and interests of the regime. The discourse of history, hardly distinguished from policy, ends up by absorbing the concerns and objectives of the latter.

In this affinity with policy historiography reveals its character as a form of *colonialist knowledge*. That is, it derives directly from that knowledge which the bourgeoisie had used in the period of their ascendancy to interpret the world in order to master it and establish their hegemony over Western societies, but turned into an instrument of national oppression as they began to acquire for themselves 'a place in the sun'. It was thus that political science which had defined the ideal of citizenship for European nation-states was used in colonial India to set up institutions and frame laws designed specifically to generate a mitigated and second-class citizenship. Political economy which had developed in Europe as a critique of feudalism was made to promote a neo-feudal landlordism in India. Historiography too adapted itself to the relations of power under the Raj and was harnessed more and more to the service of the State.

It was thanks to this connection and a good deal of talent to back it up that historical writing on themes of the colonial period shaped up as a highly coded discourse. Operating within the framework of a many-sided affirmation of British rule in the subcontinent it assumed the function of representing the recent past of its people as 'England's Work in India'. A discourse of power in its own right it had each of its moments displayed as a triumph, that is, as the most favourable upshot of a number of conflicting possibilities for the regime at any particular time. In its mature form, therefore, as in *Hunter's Annals,* continuity figures as one of its necessary and cardinal aspects. Unlike primary discourse it cannot afford to be foreshortened and without a sequel. The event does not constitute its sole content, but is the middle term between a beginning which serves as a context and an end which is at the same time a perspective linked to the next sequence. The only element that is constant in this ongoing series is the Empire and the policies needed to safeguard and perpetuate it.

Functioning as he does within this code Hunter with all the goodwill so solemnly announced in his dedicatory note ('These pages . . . have little to say touching the governing race. My business is with the people') writes up the history of a popular struggle as one in which the real subject is not the people but, indeed, 'the governing race' institutionalised as the Raj. Like any other narrative of this kind his account of the *hool* too is there to celebrate a continuity—that of British power in India. The statement of causes and reforms is no more than a structural requirement for this continuum providing it respectively with context and perspective. These serve admirably to register the event as a datum in the life-story of the Empire, but do nothing to illuminate that consciousness which is called insurgency. The rebel has no place in this history as the subject of rebellion.

XI

There is nothing in tertiary discourse to make up for this absence. Farthest removed in time from the events which it has for its theme it always looks at them in the third person. It is the work of non-official writers in most cases or of former officials no longer under any professional obligation or constraint to represent the standpoint of the government. If it happens to carry an official view at all this is only because the author has chosen it of his own will rather than because he has been conditioned to do so by any loyalty or allegiance based on administrative involvement. There are indeed some historical works which actually show such a preference and are unable to speak in a voice other than that of the custodians of law and dorder—an instance of tertiary discourse reverting to that state of crude identification with the regime so characteristic of primary discourse.

But there are other and very different idioms within this genre ranging from liberal to left. The latter is particularly important as perhaps the most influential and prolific of all the many varieties of tertiary discourse. We owe to it some of the best studies on Indian peasant insurgency and more and more of these are coming out all the time as evidence both of a growing academic interest in the subject and the relevance that the subaltern movements of the past have to contemporary tensions in our part of the world. This literature is distinguished by its effort to break away from the code of counter-insurgency. It adopts the insurgent's point of view and regards, with him, as 'fine' what the other side calls 'terrible', and vice versa. It leaves the reader in no doubt that it wants the rebels and not their enemies to win. Here unlike in secondary discourse of the liberal-imperialist type recognition of the wrongs done to the peasants leads directly to support for their struggle to seek redress by arms.

Yet these two types, so very different from and contrary to each other in ideological orientation, have much else that is common between them. Take for instance that remarkable contribution of radical scholarship. Suprakash Ray's *Bharater Krishak-bidroha O Ganatantrik Samgram*[26] and compare its account of the Santal uprising of 1855 with Hunter's. The texts echo each other as narratives. Ray's being the later work has all the advantage of drawing on more recent research such as Datta's, and thus being more informed. But much of what it has to say about the inauguration and development of the *hool* is taken—in fact, quoted directly—from Hunter's *Annals*.[27] And both the authors rely on the *Calcutta Review* (1856) article for much of their evidence. There is thus little in the description of this particular event which differs significantly between the secondary and the tertiary types of discourse.

Nor is there much to distinguish between the two in terms of their admiration for the courage of the rebels and their abhorrence of the genocidal operations mounted by the counter-insurgency forces. In fact, on both these points Ray reproduces *in extenso* Hunter's testimony, gathered first-hand from officers directly involved in the campaign, that the Santals 'did not understand yielding', while for the army, 'it was not war . . . it was execution'.[28] The sympathy expressed for the enemies of the Raj in the radical tertiary discourse is matched fully by that in the colonialist secondary discourse. Indeed, for both, the *hool* was an eminently just struggle—an evaluation derived from their mutual concurrence about the factors which had provoked it. Wicked landlords, extortionate usurers, dishonest traders, venal police, irresponsible officials and partisan processes of law—all figure with equal prominence in both the accounts. Both the historians draw on the evidence recorded on this subject in the *Calcutta Review* essay, and for much of his information about Santal indebtedness and bond slavery, about moneylenders' and landlords' oppression and administrative connivance at all this Ray relies heavily again on Hunter, as witness the extracts quoted liberally from the latter's work.[29]

However, causality is used by the two writers to develop entirely different perspectives. The statement of causes has the same part to play in Hunter's account as in any other narrative of the secondary type—that is, as an essential aspect of the discourse of counter-insurgency. In this respect his *Annals* belongs to a tradition of colonialist historiography which, for this particular event, is typically exemplified by that racist and vindicative essay, 'The Sonthal Rebellion'. There the obviously knowledgeable but tough-minded official ascribes the uprising, as Hunter does, to banias' fraud, mahajani transaction, zamindari despotism and sarkari inefficiency. In much the same vein Thornhill's *Personal Adventures* accounts for the rural uprisings of the period of the Mutiny in Uttar Pradesh quite clearly by the breakdown in traditional agrarian relations consequent on the advent of British rule. O'Malley identifies the root of the Pabna *bidroha* of 1873 in rack-renting by landlords, and the Deccan Riots Commission that of the disturbances of 1875 in the exploitation of the Kunbi peasantry by alien moneylenders in Poona and Ahmednagar districts.[30] One could go on adding many other events and texts to this list. The spirit of all these is well represented in the following extract from the *judicial Department Resolutions* of 22 November 1831 on the subject of the insurrection led by Titu Mir:

> The serious nature of the late disturbances in the district of Baraset renders it an object of paramount importance that the *cause* which gave rise to them should be fully *investigated* in order that the motives which activated the insurgents may be rightly *understood* and such measures adopted as may be deemed expedient to *prevent a recurrence of similar disorders.*[31]

That sums it up. To know the cause of a phenomenon is already a step taken in the direction of controlling it. To *investigate* and thereby *understand* the cause of rural disturbances is an aid to measures 'deemed expedient to *prevent a recurrence of similar disorders*'. To that end the correspondent of the *Calcutta Review* (1856) recommended 'that condign retribution', namely, 'that they [the Santals] should be surrounded and hunted up everywhere . . . . that they should be compelled, by force, if need be, to return to the Damin-i-koh, and to the wasted country in Bhaugulpore and Beerbhoom, to rebuild the ruined villages, restore the desolate fields to cultivation, open roads, and advance general public works; and do this under watch and guard . . . . and that this state of things should be continued, until they are completely tranquillised, and reconciled to their allegiance.'[32] The gentler alternative put forward by Hunter was, as we have seen, a combination of Martial Law to suppress an ongoing revolt and measures to follow it up by 'English enterprise' in order (as his compatriot had suggested) to absorb the unruly peasantry as a cheap labour force in agriculture and public works for the benefit respectively of the same *dikus* and railway and road work engineers against whom they had taken up arms. With all their variation in tone, however, both the prescriptions to 'make . . . rebellion impossible by the elevation of the Sonthals'[33] — indeed, all colonialist solutions arrived at by the casual explanation of our peasant uprisings—were grist to a historiography committed to assimilating them to the transcendental Destiny of the British Empire.

XII

Causality serves to hitch the *hool* to a rather different kind of Destiny in Ray's account. But the latter goes through the same steps as Hunter's—that is, *context-event-perspective* ranged along a historical continuum—to arrive there. There are some obvious parallelisms in the way the event acquires a context in the two works. Both start off with prehistory (treated more briefly by Ray than Hunter) and follow it up with a survey of the more recent past since 1790 when the tribe first came into contact with the regime. It is there that the cause of the insurrection lies for both—but with a difference. For Hunter the disturbances originated in a local malignance in an otherwise healthy body—the failure of a district administration to act up to the then emerging ideal of the Raj as the *ma-baap* of the peasantry and protect them from the tyranny of wicked elements within the native society itself. For Ray it was the very presence of British power in India which had goaded the Santals to revolt, for their enemies the landlords and moneylenders owed their authority and indeed their existence to the new arrangements in landed property introduced by the colonial government and the accelerated development of a money economy under its impact. The rising constituted, therefore, a critique not only of a local administration but of colonialism itself. Indeed he uses Hunter's own evidence to arrive at that very different, indeed contrary, conclusion:

> It is clearly proved by Hunter's own statement that the responsibility for the extreme misery of the Santals lies with the English administrative system taken as a whole together with the zamindars and mahajans. For it was the English administrative system which had created zamindars and mahajans in order to satisfy its own need for exploitation and government, and helped them directly and indirectly by offering its protection and patronage.[34]

With colonialism that is, the Raj as system and in its entirety (rather than any of its local malfunctions) identified thus as the prime cause of rebellion, its outcome acquires radically different values in the two texts. While Hunter is explicit in his preference of a victory in favour of the regime;

Ray is equally so infavour of the rebels. And corresponding to this each has a perspective which stands out in sharp contrast to that of the other. It is for Hunter the consolidation of British rule based on a reformed administration which no longer incites jacqueries by its failure to protect *adivasis* from native exploiters, but transforms them into an abundant and mobile labour force readily and profitably employed by Indian landlords and 'English enterprise'. For Ray the event is 'the precursor of the great rebellion' of 1857 and a vital link in a protracted struggle of the Indian people in general and peasants and workers in particular against foreign as well as indigenous oppressors. The armed insurrection of the Santals, he says, has indicated a way to the Indian people. 'That particular way has, thanks to the great rebellion of 1857, developed into the broad highway of India's struggle for freedom. That highway extends into the twentieth century. The Indian peasantry are on their march along that very highway.'[35] In fitting the *hool* thus to a perspective of continuing struggle of the rural masses the author draws on a well-established tradition of radical historiography as witness, for instance, the following extract from a pamphlet which had a wide readership in left political circles nearly thirty years ago:

> The din of the actual battles of the insurrection has died down. But its echoes have kept on vibrating through the years, growing louder and louder as more peasants joined in the fight. The clarion call that summoned the Santhals to battle. . . was to be heard in other parts of the country at the time of the Indigo Strike of 1860, the Pabna and Bogra Uprising of 1872, the Maratha Peasant Rising in Poona and Ahmednagar in 1875-76. It was finally to merge in the massive demand of the peasantry all over the country for an end to zamindari and moneylending oppression . . . Glory to the immortal Santhals who . . . . showed the path to battle! The banner of militant struggle has since then passed from hand to hand over the length and breadth of India.[36]

The power of such assimilative thinking about the history of peasant insurgency is further illustrated by the concluding words of an essay written by a veteran of the peasant movement and published by the Pashchimbanga Pradeshik

Krishak Sabha on the eve of the centenary of the Santal revolt. Thus,

> The flames of the fire kindled by the peasant martyrs of the Santal insurrection a hundred years ago had spread to many regions all over India. Those flames could be seen burning in the indigo cultivators' rebellion in Bengal (1860), in the uprising of the raiyats of Pabna and Bogra (1872), in that of the Maratha peasantry of the Deccan (1875-76). The same fire was kindled again and again in the course of the Moplah peasant revolts of Malabar. That fire has not been extinguished yet, it is still burning in the hearts of the Indian peasants. . . [37]

The purpose of such tertiary discourse is quite clearly to try and retrieve the history of insurgency from that continuum which is designed to assimilate every jacquerie to 'England's Work in India' and arrange it along the alternative axis of a protracted campaign for freedom and socialism. However, as with colonialist historiography this, too, amounts to an act of appropriation which excludes the rebel as the conscious subject of his own history and incorporates the latter as only a contingent element in another history with another subject. Just as it is not the rebel but the Raj which is the real subject of secondary discourse and the Indian bourgeoisie that of tertiary discourse of the History-of-the-Freedom-Struggle genre, so is an *abstraction* called Worker-and-Peasant, *an ideal rather than the real historical personality of the insurgent,* made to replace him in the type of literature discussed above.

To say this is of course not to deny the political importance of such appropriation. Since every struggle for power by the historically ascendant classes in any epoch involves a bid to acquire a tradition, it is entirely in the fitness of things that the revolutionary movements in India should lay a claim to, among others, the Santal rebellion of 1855 as a part of their heritage. But however noble the cause and instrument of such appropriation, it leads to the mediation of the insurgent's consciousness by the historian's—that is, of a past consciousness by one conditioned by the present. The distortion which follows necessarily and inevitably from this process is a function of that hiatus between event-time and discourse-time which makes the verbal representation of the past less than accurate in the best of cases. And since the discourse is, in this particular instance, one about properties of the mind-about attitudes, beliefs, ideas, etc. rather than about externalities which are easier to identify and describe, the task of representation is made even more complicated than usual.

There is nothing that historiography can do to eliminate such distortion altogether, for the latter is built into its optics. What is can do, however, is to acknowledge such distortion as parametric—as a datum which determines the form of the exercise itself, and to stop pretending that it can *fully* grasp a past consciousness and reconstitute it. Then and only then might the distance between the latter and the historian's perception of it be reduced significantly enough to amount to a close approximation which is the best one could hope for. The gap as it stands at the moment is indeed so wide that there is much more than an irreducible degree of error in the existing literature on this point. Even brief look at some of the discourses on the 1855 insurrection should bear this out.

XIII

Religiosity was, by all accounts, central to the *hool*. The notion of power which inspired it, was made up of such ideas and expressed in such words and acts as were explicitly religious in character. It was not that power was a content wrapped up in a form external to it called religion. It was a matter of both being inseparably collapsed as the signified and its signifier (*vāgarthāviva samprktau)* in the language of that massive violence. Hence the attribution of the rising to a divine command rather than to any particular grievance; the enactment of rituals both before (e.g. propitiatory ceremonies to ward off the apocalypse of the Primeval Serpents—Lag and Lagini, the distribution of *tel-sindur,* etc.) and during the uprising (e.g. worshipping the goddess Durga, bathing in the Ganges, etc.); the generation and circulation of myth in its characteristic vehicle—rumour (e.g. about the advent of 'the exterminating angel' incarnated as a buffalo, the birth of a prodigious hero to a virgin, etc.)[38] The evidence is both unequivocal and ample on this point. The statements we have from the leading protagonists and their followers are all emphatic and indeed isistent on this aspect of their struggle, as should be obvious even from the few extracts of source material reproduced below in the *Appendix*. In sum, it is not possible to speak of insurgency in this case except as a religious consciousness—except, that is, as a massive demonstration of self-estrangement (to borrow Marx's term for the very essence of religiosity) which made the rebels look upon their project as predicated on a will other than their own: 'Kanoo and Seedoo Manjee are not fighting. The Thacoor himself will fight.'[39]

How authentically has this been represented in historical discourse? It was identified in official correspondence at the time as a case of 'fanaticism'. The insurrection was three months old and still going strong when J. R. Ward, a Special Commissioner and one of the most important administrators in the Birbhum region, wrote in some desperation to his superiors in Calcutta, 'I have been unable to trace the insurrection in Beerbhoom to any thing but *fanaticism*'. The idiom he used to describe the phenomenon was typical of the shocked and culturally arrogant response of nineteenth-century colonialism to any radical movement inspired by a non-Christian doctrine among a subject population: 'These Sonthals have been led to join in the rebellion under a persuasion which is clearly traceable to their brethren in Bhaugulpore, that an Almighty & inspired Being appeared as the redeemer of their Caste & their *ignorance & superstition* was easily worked into a *religious frenzy* which has stopped at nothing.'[40] That idiom occurs also in the *Calcutta Review* article. There the Santal is acknowledged as 'an eminently religious man and his revolt as a parallel of other historical occasions when *'the fanatical spirit of religious superstition'* had been 'swayed to strengthen and help forward a quarrel already ready to burst and based on other grounds.'[41] However, the author gives this identification a significantly different slant from that in the report quoted above. There an incomprehending Ward, caught in the blast of the *hool*, appears to have been impressed by the spontaneity of 'a religious frenzy which . . . . stopped at nothing'. By contrast the article written after the regime had recovered its self-confidence, thanks to the search-and-burn campaign in the disturbed tracts, interprets religiosity as a propagandist ruse used by the leaders to sustain the morale of the rebels. Referring, for instance, to the messianic rumours in circulation it says, 'All these absurdities were no doubt *devised* to keep up the courage of the numerous rabble.'[42] Nothing could be more elitist. The insurgents are regarded here as a mindless 'rabble' devoid of a will of their own and easily manipulated by their chiefs.

But elitism such as this is not a feature of colonialist historiography alone. Tertiary discourse of the radical variety, too, exhibits the same disdain for the political consciousness of the peasant masses when it is mediated by religiosity. For a sample let us turn to Ray's account of the ring again. He quotes the following lines from the *Calcutta Review* article in a somewhat inaccurate but still clearly recognizable translation:

> Seedoo and Kanoo were at night seated in their home, revolving many things. . . a bit of paper fell on Seedoo's head, and suddenly the Thakoor (God) appeared before the astonished gaze of Seedoo and Kanoo; he was like a white man though dressed in the native style; on each hand he had ten fingers; he held a white book, and wrote therein; the book and with it 20 pieces of paper. . . he presented to the brothers; ascended upwards, and disappeared. Another bit of paper fell on Seedoo's head, and then came two men. . . hinted to them the purport of Thakoor's order, and they likewise vanished. But there was not merely one apparition of the sublime Thakoor; each day in the week for some short period, did he make known his presence to his favourite apostles . . . . In the silvery pages of the book, and upon the white leaves of the single scraps of paper, were words written; these were afterwards deciphered by literate Sonthals, able to read and interpret; but their meaning had already been sufficiently indicated to the two leaders. [43]

With some minor changes of detail (inevitable in a living folklore) this is indeed a fairly authentic account of the visions the two Santal leaders believed they had. Their statements, reproduced in part in the *Appendix* (Extracts 3 and 4), bear this out. These, incidentally, were not public pronouncements meant to impress their followers. Unlike 'The Thacoor's Perwannah' (*Appendix*: Extract 2) intended to make their views known to the authorities before the uprising these were the words of captives facing execution. Addressed to hostile interrogators in military encampments they could have little use as propaganda. Uttered by men of a tribe which, according to all accounts had not yet learnt to lie,[44] these represented the truth and nothing but the truth for their speakers. But that is not what Ray would credit them with. What figures as a mere insinuation in the *Calcutta Review* is raised to the status of an elaborate propaganda device in his introductory remarks on the passage cited above. Thus:

> Both Sidu and Kanu knew that the slogan (*dhawani*) which would have the most effect among the *backward* Santals, was one that was religious. Therefore, *in order to inspire* the Santals to struggle the *spread* the word about God's directive in favour of launching such a struggle. The story *invented (kalpita)* by them is as follows.[45]

There is little that is different here from what the colonialist writer had to say about the presumed backwardness of the Santal peasantry, the manipulative designs of their leaders and the uses of religion as the means of such manipulation. Indeed, on each of these points Ray does better and is by far the more explicit of the two authors in attributing a gross lie and downright deception to the rebel chiefs without any evidence at all. The invention is all his own and testifies to the failure of a shallow radicalism to conceptualise insurgent mentality except in terms of an unadulterated secularism. Unable to grasp religiosity as the central modality of peasant consciousness in colonial India he is shy to acknowledge its mediation of the peasant's idea of power and all the resultant contradictions. He is obliged therefore to rationalise the ambiguities of rebel politics by assigning a worldly consciousness to the leaders and an otherworldly one to their followers making of the latter innocent dupes of crafty men armed with all the tricks of a modern Indian politician out to solicit rural votes. Where this lands the historian can be seen even more clearly the projection of this thesis to a study of the Birsaite *ulgulan* in Ray's subsequent work. He writes,

> In order to propagate this religious doctrine of his Birsa adopted a *new device (kaushal)*—just as Sidu, the Santal

leader, had done on the eve of the Santal rebellion of 1885. Birsa knew that the Kol were a *very backward* people and were full of *religious superstition* as a result of Hindu-Brahmanical and Christian missionary propaganda amongst them over a long period. Therefore, it would not doto avoid the question of religion if the Kol people were to be liberated from those wicked religious influences and drawn into the path of rebellion. Rather, in order to overcome the evil influences of Hindu and Christian religions, it would be necessary to spread his new religious faith among them in the name of that very God of theirs, and to introduce new rules. *To this end, recourse had to be had to falsehood, if necessary, in the interests of the people.*

Birsa *spread* the word that he had received this new religion of his from the chief deity of the Mundas, Sing Bonga, himself.[46]

Thus the radical historian is driven by the logic of his own incomprehension to attribute a deliberate falsehood to one of the greatest of our rebels. The ideology of that mighty *ulgulan* is nothing but pure fabrication for him. And he is not alone in his misreading of insurgent consciousness. Baskay echoes him almost word for word in describing the Santal leader's claim to divine support for the *hool* as propaganda meant 'to inspire the Santals to rise in revolt'.[47] Formulations such as these have their foil in other writings of the same genre which solve the riddle of religious thinking amogn the Santal rebels by ignoring it altogether. A reader who has Natarajan's and Rasul' once influential essays as his only source of information about the insurrection of 1855, would hardly suspect any religiosity at all in that great event. It is represented there *exclusively* in its secular aspects. This attitude is of course not confined to the authors discussed in this essay. The same mixture of myopia and downright refusal to look at the evidence that is there, characterises a great deal more of the existing literature on the subject.

XIV

Why is tertiary discourse, even of the radical variety, so reluctant to come to terms with the religious element in rebel consciousness? Because it is still trapped in the paradigm which inspired the ideologically contrary, because colonialist, discourse of the primary and secondary types. It follows, in each case, from a refusal to acknowledge the insurgent as the subject of his own history. For once a peasant rebellion has been assimilated to the carrier of the Raj, the Nation or the People, it becomes easy for the historian to abdicate the responsibility he has of exploring and describing the consciousness specific to that rebellion and be content to ascribe to it a transcendental consciousness. In operative terms, this means denying a will to the mass of the rebels themselves and representing them merely as instruments of some other will. It is thus that in colonialist historiography insurgency is seen as the articulation of a pure spontaneity pitted against the will to the State as embodied in the Raj. If any consciousness is attributed at all to the rebels, it is only a few of their leaders—more often than not some individual members or small groups of the gentry—who are credited with it. Again, in bourgeois—nationalist historiography it is an elite consciousness which is read into all peasant movements as their motive force. This had led to such grotesqueries as the characterisation of the Indigo Rebellion of 1860 as 'the first non-violent mass movement'[48] and generally of all the popular struggles in rural India during the first hundred and twentyfive years of British rule as the spiritual harbinger of the Indian National Congress.

In much the same way the specificity of rebel consciousness had eluded radical historiography as well. This has been so because it is impaled on a concept of peasant revolts as a succession of events ranged along a direct line of descent—as a heritage, as it is often called—in which all the constituent have the same pedigree and replicate another in their commitment to the highest ideals of liberty, equality and fraternity. In this historical view of the history of insurgency all moments of consciousness are assimilated to the ultimate and highest moment of the series—indeed to an Ideal Consciousness. A historiography devoted to its pursuit (even when that is done, regrettably, in the name of Marxism) is ill-equipped to cope with contradictions which are indeed the stuff history is made of. Since the Ideal is suppose to be one hundred per cent secular in character, the devotee tends to look away when confronted with the evidence of religiosity as if the latter did not exist or explain it away as a clever but well-intentioned fraud perpetrated by enlightened leaders on their moronic followers—all done, of course, 'in the interests of the people'! Hence, the rich material of myths, rituals, rumours, hopes for a Golden Age and fears of an imminent End of the World, all of which speaks of the self-alienation of the rebel, is wasted on this abstract and sterile discourse. It can do little to illuminate that combination of sectarianism and militancy which is so important a feature of our rural history. The ambiguity of such phenomena, witnessed during the Tebhaga movement in Dinajpur, as Muslim peasants comign to the Kisan Sabha 'sometimes inscribing a hammer or a sickle on the Muslim League flag' and young maulavis 'creciting melödious verse from the Koran' at village meetings as 'they condemned the jotedari system and the practice of charging high interest rates',[49] will be beyond its grasp. The swift transformation of class struggle into communal strife and vice versa in our countryside evokes from it either some well-contrived apology or a simple gesture of embarrassment, but no real explanation.

However, it is not only the religious element in rebel consciousness which this historiography fails to comprehend. The specificity of a rural insurrection is expressed in terms of many other contradictions as well. These too are missed out. Blinded by the glare of a perfect and immaculate consciousness the historian sees nothing, for instance, but solidarity in rebel behaviour and fails to notice its other, namely, betrayal. Committed inflexibly to the notion of insurgency as a generalised movement, he underestimates the power of the brakes put on it by localism and territoriality. Convinced that mobilisation for a rural uprising flows exclusively from an overall elite authority, he tends to disregard the operation of many other authorities within the primordial relations of a rural community. A prisoner of empty abstractions tertiary discourse, even of the radical kind, has thus distanced itself from the prose of counter-insurgency only by a declaration of sentiment so far. It has still to go a long way before it can prove that the insurgent can rely on its performance to recover his place in history.

Abbreviations

BC: Board's Collections, India Office Records (London).
JC: Fort William Judicial Consultations in BC.
JP: Judicial Proceedings, West Bengal State Archieves (Calcutta).
MDS: *Maharaja Deby Sinha* (Nashipur Raj Estate, 1914).

NOTES

1. I am grateful to my colleagues of the editorial team for their comments on an initial draft of this essay.

2. The instances are far too numerous to cite. For some of these see *MDS*, pp. 46-7, 48-9 on the Rangpur *dhing*; BC 54222 Metcalfe & Blunt to Court of Directors (10 April 1832), paras 14-15 on the Barasat uprising; W. W. Hunter, *Annals of Rural Bengal* (7th edition; London, 1897), pp. 237-8 and JP, 4 Oct. 1855; 'The Thacoor's Perwannah' for the Santal *hool* C.E. Buckland, *Bengal Under the Lieutenant-Governors*, vol. I (Calcutta, 1901), p. 192 for the 'blue mutiny'.

3. See, for instance, *MDS*, pp. 579-80; *Freedom Struggle in Uttar Pradesh*, vol. IV (Lucknow, 1959), pp. 284-5,549).

4. J. C Price, *The Chuar Rebellion of 1799*, p. cl. The edition of the work used in this essay is the one printed in A. Mitra (ed.) *District Handbooks: Midnapur* (Alipore, 1953), Appendix IV.

5. BC 54222: *JC*, 22 Nov. 1831: Extract from the Proceedings of the Honourable the Vice President in Council in the Military Department under date the 10th November 1831'. Emphasis added.

6. *JP*, 19 July 1855: Enclosure to letter from the Magistrate of Murshidabad, dated 11 July 1855. Emphasis added.

7. Thus, BC 54222: *JC*, 3 Apr. 1832: Alexander to Barwell (28 Nov. 1831).

8. My debt to Roland Barthes for many of the analytic terms and procedures used in this section and generally throughout this essay should be far too obvious to all familiar with his 'Structural Analysis of Narratives' and 'The struggle with the Angel' in Barthes, *Image-Music-Text* (Glasgow, 1977), pp. 79-141, and 'Historical Discourse' in M. Lane (ed.) , *Structuralism, A Reader*

(London, 1970), pp. 145-55, to require detailed reference except where I quote directly from this literature.

9. Barthes, *Images-Music-Text,* p. 102.

10. Emile Benveniste, *Problems de linguistique generale,* I (Paris, 1966), p. 126. The original dissociation nous livre la constitution formelle; I' intégration nous live des unités significantes', has been rendered somewhat differently and I feel, less happily, in the English translation of the work, *Problems in General Linguistics* (Florida, 1971), p. 107.

11. Barthes, *Image-Music-Text,* p. 93.

12. Charles Bally, *Linguistique Générale et Linguistique Francaise* (Berne, 1965), p.144.

13. Barthes, *Elements of Semiology* (London, 1967), p. 60.

14. Barthes, *Image-Music-Text,* p. 128.

15. Ibid, p. 119.

16. *Selected Works of Mao Tse-tung,* vol. I (Peking, 1967), pp. 26-7.

17. Benveniste, op. cit. , p. 239.

18. *Freedom Struggle in Uttar Pradesh* vol. V. pp. 685-92.

19. For Roman Jakobson's exposition of this key concept, see his *Selected Writings, 2: Word and Language* (The Hague and Paris, 1971), pp. 130-47. Barthes develops the notion of organisation shifters in his essay 'Historical Discourse, pp. 146-8. All extract quoted in this paragraph are taken from that essay unless otherwise mentioned.

20. Price, op. cit. , p. clx.

21. Ibid.

22. Reginald G. Wilberforce, *An Unrecorded Chapter of the Indian Mutiny* (2nd edition; London, 1894), pp. 76-7.

23. It appears from a note in this work that parts of it were written in 1866. The dedication bears the date 4 March 1868. All our references to this work in quotation or otherwise are to Chapter IV of the seventh edition (London, 1897) unless otherwise stated. p. 112.

24. Barthes, *Image-Music-Text,* p. 112.

25. Anon., 'The Sonthal Rebellion', *Calcutta Review* (856), 223-64; K.

K. Datta, 'The Santal Insurrection', in *Anti-British Plots and Movements before 1857* (Meerut, 1970), pp. 43-152.

26. Vol. I (Calcutta, 1966), Ch. 13.

27. For these see ibid., 323, 325, 327, 328.

28. Ibid,. p. 337 Hunter, op. cit., pp. 247-9.

29. Ray, op. cit., pp. 316-19.

30. Anon., op. cit., pp. 238-41; Thornhill, op. cit., pp. 33-5; L.S.S. O'Malley, *Bengal District Gazetteers: Pabna* (Calcutta, 1923), p. 25; *Report of the Commission Appointed in India to Inquire into the Causes of the Riots which took place in the year 1875 in the Poona and Ahmednagar District of the Bombay Presidency* (London, 1878), Passim.

31. BC 54222: *JC*, 22 Nov. 1831. (no. 91) Emphasis added.

32. Anon., op. cit., pp. 263-4.

33. Ibid., p. 263.

34. Ray, op. cit., p. 318.

35. Ibid., p. 340.

36. L. Natarajan, *Peasant Uprisings in India, 1850-1900* (Bombay, 1953), pp. 31-2.

37 Abdullah Rasul, *Santal Bidroher Amar Kahini* (Calcutta, 1954), p. 24.

38. The instances are far too numerous to cite in an essay of this size, but for some samples see *Mare Hapram Ko Reak Katha, Ch. 79, in A. Mitra (ed.), District Handbooks: Bankura* (Calcutta, 1953).

39. *Appendix:* Extract 2.

40. *JP*, 8 Nov. 1855: Ward to Government of Bengal (13 Oct., 1855). Emphasis added.

41. Anon., op. cit., p. 243. Emphasis added.

42. Ibid., p. 246, Emphasis added.

43. Ibid., pp. 243-4, Ray, op. cit., pp. 321-2.

44. This is generally accepted. See, for instance, Sherwill's observation about the truth being sacred to the Santals offering in this respect a bright example to their lying neighbours, the Bengalis'. *Geographical and Statistical Report of the District Bhaugulpoor* (Calcutta, 1854), p. 32.

45. Ray, op. cit., p. 321. Emphasis added.

46. Ray, *Bharater Baiplabik Samgramer Itihas,* vol. I (Calcutta, 1970), p. 95. Emphasis added. The sentence italicized by us in the quoted passage reads as follows in the Bengali original: *'Eijanyo prayojan boiley jatir svarthey mithyar asroy grahan karitey hoibey.'*

47. Dhirendranath Baskay, *Saontal Ganasamgramer Itihas* (Calcutta, 1976), p. 66.

48. Jogesh Chandra Bagal (ed.), *Peasant Revolution in Bengal* (Calcutta, 1953), p. 5.

49. Sunil Sen, *Agrarian Struggle in Bengal, 1946-47* (New Delhi, 1972), p. 49.

CHAPTER 6

The Economic Background of Communalism in India

'Honest communalism is fear; false communalism is political reaction . . . Social and economic forces will inevitably bring other problems to the front. They will create cleavages along different lines, but the communal cleavage will go.'

Jawaharlal Nehru *Recent Essays and Writings* (Allahabad, 1937), pp. 51, 61.

'Communalism has as its causes many and intricate factors: economic, religious, psychological and so on. The question as to which of these factors is the most important presumably means *which is the most accessible to change*. Given any other meaning, the question is both unanswerable and unimportant'.

Wilfred Cantwell Smith, *Modern Islam in India: A Social Analysis* (Lahore, 1969), p. 188.

'The background of the men who organised the campaign (for Pakistan) was not theology and Islamic law but politics and the common law, not Deoband but Cambridge and the Inns of Court. Mr. Jinnah and his lieutenants such as Liaquat Ali won Pakistan largely in spite of men of religion. They led a secular campaign to create a state based on religion.

Keith Callard, *Pakistan, A Political Study* (London, 1958), p. 200.

I

Historians have generally asserted that the roots of the present lie deep in the past and an adequate understanding of the present is not possible without an understanding of the past. What has often been overlooked is that the understanding of the past itself may remain partial without reference to the present.[1] What is more important, sometimes traumatic developments in the present may shed an entirely new light on the past; they may even compel a thorough re-appraisal of the earlier views and interpretations of past history.

The historian who is inclined to assert that in the political evolution of modern India no single element has been as pervasive as religion[2] or that the root of political polarisation in India was the religious antipathy between Hindus and Muslims'[3], seems to be guilty of exaggerating the significance of the religious factor. That this statement ignores certain other powerful forces that have shaped (and are shaping) the history of modern Indian becomes glaringly manifest when viewed in the light of recent events in the Indian subcontinent. The break-up of Pakistan and the emergence of sovereign Bangladesh should give a rude jolt to even the most dogmatic exponents of 'religious' interpretations of modern Indian history. Recent events make it necessary to take a fresh look at the past and to re-assess the interplay of the religious and non-religious factors in the growth of communalism in India.

It must be noted that the study of communalism from a macro-sociological or political-economic standpoint has not yet emerged as an important field of inquiry in social science research.

Explanations of the communal problem have been biased in favour of either the religious, the economic, or the political factors. Very rarely does one come across explanations which attempt to investigate the kind of political-economic, framework or background in which the factor of past religious antipathy developed into a force of explosive potentialities. In other words, very rarely does one come across an attempt to evolve a comprehensive and integrated approach to the problem. This weakness has originated both from a lack of adequate theoretical perspective and of poverty of authentic empirical material collected through painstaking investigation.

It may be noted, further, that at different times different interpretations of communalism have been fashionable among the thinking sections of Indian society. These interpretations have emanated from the political and psychological pressures of historical situations rather than from serious and systematic inquiry into actual facts and events. In fact, far from showing an awareness of political biases and preconceptions, and evolving a scientific approach to the problem, social scientists themselves have acted as partisans of one view or the other. Bias has most often assumed the form of ignoring altogether the problem of communalism as a scientists problem. Thus recent studies of social change or politics in India[4] have generally avoided grappling with the problem of communalism. In this context, recent political developments in the Indian subcontinent also have a great significance for social science. They provide a favourable context for questioning many established dogmas, assumptions and hypotheses which have been current in the past among Indian and non-Indian scholars of diverse ideological persuasions. It should also be indicated that sociological and political thought in Western countries is rich in approaches and insights on the social and economic roots of conservatism. Looking at communalism as an extreme form of conservatism in the context of the Indian subcontinent, an exploration to the roots of communalism should also provide an opportunity for appraising the relevance of Western approaches, concepts and categories for a study of this problem.[5]

The present chapter aims mainly at posing certain general issues on the question of the economic basis of the communal problem in the pre-independence period. It should be treated as only an attempt to clarify certain questions of approach and to formulate a plausible hypothesis on this subject.

II

A scientific treatment of the problem of communalism first requires clarification of the basic approach to this problem. In the past, the approach adopted by many scholars was dichotomous rather than dialectical, static rather than dynamic, partial rather than comprehensive. There has been a tendency among one group of scholars to treat one set of factors as causes and the other set as effects; other scholars have, on the other hand, been inclined to treat a different set of factors as causes and the other set as effects.[6] This bias for a 'single factor' or 'a basic factor' explanation does not allow for dynamic interaction between all the *relevant* factors or for what Myrdal calls the press of 'Cumulative Causation'[7] in producing a phenomenon like communalism. The conventional type of analysis of communalism thus fails to grasp that 'the essence of a social problem is that it concerns a complex of inter-locking, circular and cumulative changes'.[8]

More concretely, the explanations of communalism in terms of a 'clash of cultures and a conflict over the distribution of power'[9] do not adequately explain why in certain periods or situations, this conflict has been accentuated, what have been the motivating forces of this conflict and what the relationship between the cultural or power situation on the one hand and the economic situation on the other. Similarly, an explanation of communalism in terms either of a cloak for the struggle between Hindu and Muslim vested interests or as a distorted expression of conflicts between the exploiters and the exploited fails to explain fully the conditions and mechanisms which promote an intermeshing of religion and economics, or a distortion of the economic question by religion in Indina life. In other words, a satisfactory explanation of communalism presupposes a conceptual framework which helps in relating one set of factors with another and in presenting a more sophisticated analysis of the causal nexus.

It should be noted that the explanation of political cleavage in terms of religious antipathy between Hindus and Muslims is not a causal explanation but a tautology. As far as the element of religious antipathy is concerned, it is a carry-over from a previous historical situation. Why is it that the seed of *religious* antipathy carried over from the pre-British period developed under British rule into a full-fledged *political* antagonism on religious lines? It should be noted, further, that the history of Hindu-Muslim relations in the pre-British period was a history both of antipathy and of reconciliation. If in the later period the element of antipathy got the upper hand and became the basis for communal cleavage, the cause of this must be sought not only in the peculiarly resilient character of this antipathy, but also in the interplay of new forces during the period of British rule.

The history of many countries bears testimony to the fact that the dead past—with all its memories, myths and legends—comes to life only in relation to problems and compulsions of the living present.[10] In this context, it can be argued that religion in the form of communalism did not emerge as a great divisive force under British rule in India as a projection or continuation of past history. It was the intensification of conflicts over material interests resulting from the British impact, which provided an impetus for the transformation of religious antipathy during the pre-British period into a sharp political antagonism on religious lines under British rule. In short, a satisfactory answer to the Hindu-Muslim question cannot be given only in terms of past divergences of religious attitudes, beliefs and traditions. What is required for this purpose is an analysis of how these divergences affected the responses of the two communities to the economic and political challenges in different phases of British rule. In other words, for an understanding of the changes in Hindu-Muslim relations under the British, one must go beyond the sphere of religion and explore the spheres of economics and politics.

Some attempts (if not vary thorough and systematic) have been made in the past to approach the problem of communalism from this standpoint, and have yielded fruitful insights. In explaining the genesis of the communal problem, many writers have attached great importance to the fact that there existed a *lag* in modernisation among Hindus and Muslim and it was this lag which created the basis for Hindu-Muslim conflict. The lag itself is said to have arisen from the much stronger hold of conservatism or of feudal modes of thought on Muslims, which delayed, if not thwarted, their response to the challenges created by British rule. Jawaharlal Nehru, one of the foremost exponents of this view, observes:

> There has been a difference of a generation or more in the development of the Hindu and Muslim middle classes and that difference continues to show itself in many directions, political, economic and other. It is this lag which produces a psychology of fear among the Muslims.[11]

Nehru, therefore, defines communalism as essentially 'a middle class problem'. He views it as 'a narrow group mentality basing itself on a religious community but in reality concerned with political power and patronage for the interested group'.[12]

Rajni Palme Dutt, in his *India Today,* also tries to analyse the communal problem in relation to the 'socio-economic rivalry which affects the rising middle class.'[13] He also tries to show the economic basis of communal conflicts. Dutt observes:

> Behind the communal antagonisms. . . . lie social and economic questions. This is obvious in the case of the middle class communalist competing for positions and jobs. It is not less true where communal conflicts reach the masses. In Bengal and the Punjab the Hindus included the richer landlord, trading and money-lending interests; the Muslims are more often the poorer peasants and debtors. In other cases, big Muslim landlords will be found among the Hindu peasants. Again and again what is reported as a 'communal struggle' or rising conceals a struggle of Muslim peasants against Hindu landlords, Muslim debtors against Hindu money-lenders or Hindu workers against imported Pathan strike-breakers.[14]

Another important scholar, A. R. Desai, also takes note of the fact that 'a modern intelligentsia, a modern educated middle class and a bourgeoisie, on a substantial scale, sprang from within the Muslim community later than from within the Hindu community.'[15] As a result, Desai explains, the Muslims found the Hindus:

> Already firmly established in government services, as also in key positions in trade, industry and finance. They needed the support of the mass of their community in their struggle with the Hindu rivals for jobs and industrial and trade interests. They mis-directed this struggle between the sections of the same classes, as communal, as those between the Hindu community and the Muslim community.[16]

The above explanations represent a significant advance towards a new understanding of communalism by focusing on the concrete *political-economic* circumstances of the conflicts between Hindus and Muslims. It should be admitted, however, that they do not attempt to explore these circumstances in sufficient depth to adequately explain why the relations between Hindus and Muslims assumed a sharply antagonistic character and why their conflicts acquired an explosive power.

In our view, what explains this sharp antagonism between Hindus and Muslims is not just the fact of lag in social and economic development between the two communities. It is the fact that for the major part of British rule and in the key areas of the Indian sub-continent the Muslim upper class steadily *lost ground* to the Hindus.[17] Among the Hindus, in contrast, while the old type of purely feudal classes lost their eminent positions, new types of quasi-capitalist, bureaucratic and professional social strata emerged to replenish and strengthen the upper class. To use Myrdal's phraseology, while the Hindu community experienced the 'backwash' as well as the 'spread effects'[18] of the modernisation process under British rule, the Muslim community was exposed largely to the 'backwash' effects of the British impact alone. What we witness in the *psychological* sphere as the intensification of the communal consciousness is thus a sharp defensive reaction to the traumatic reverses and frustrations experienced by the Muslims in the political-economic or *material* sphere. This background helps us understand why the cry of an all-round threat to Muslim interests and the demand for a homeland for the Muslims emanated from the Muslim elite. That it also gathered support and sympathy from many other sections of the community in the later period shows not only the amenability of religion for political mobilisation. It also shows that even the lower sections of the Muslims were adversely affected by the British impact; and that they were drawn through the increasing role of the money economy, into a network of exploitation and domination by a moneyed class which happened to be Hindu. The demand for a separate homeland seemed to give an outlet to the anxieties, fears, uncertainties and aspirations of large sections of Muslims who identified 'Hindu' domination as the greatest impediment to their progress.

The growth of Muslim communalism provides a very pertinent illustration of the working of the law of 'cumulative causation'. Certain initial factors cause a set-back for the Muslims in the economic and political sphere and this set-back in turn becomes a re-inforcing factor, leading to further, and much greater handicaps and impediments to social and economic advance. As a consequence, the gap between the two communities, especially between its top classes, rapidly widens, leading to a reversal of their original positions. At the psychological level the sense of disparity and deprivation acquires an explosive power, creating a climate favouring secessionist demands. The road which led to the achievement of a homeland for the Muslims also seemed to provide a shortcut to economic and social progress.

It should be noted, however, that the problem of Hindu-Muslim relations and the character of the Muslim response to the challenges posed by British rule was not uniform in all the regions of the country. Broadly speaking , this problem assumed one form in areas like Uttar Pradesh and Bihar where Muslim upper class dominance was steadily eroded by the emergence of a new middle class from the Hindu community. It assumed an entirely different character in other regions like Bengal and Jammu-Kashmir, where a Muslim middle class was emerging from *below* and was beginning to challenge the dominance of the Hindu upper class. In the former, where the new Muslim elite was recruited largely from the landed aristocracy, the Muslim political response assumed a fanatical and negative form, the corner-stone of which was the actuate sense of envy and rivalry in relation to the Hindu community. On the other hand, in Bengal and Kashmir, where the emerging Muslim middle class was of a non-feudal origin, the political response of this class was positive and even secular in content; it had a more rational approach towards the problems of economic and social backwardness.

In short, the response of the Muslim community to the British impact crystallised into not one, but several patterns in different regions of the country. It would be wrong therefore to talk of a single response-pattern among the Muslims during British rule: it would be more realistic to talk of a plurality of response-patterns. These divergent patterns are related to the diversity of the economic and political circumstances confronting the Muslims in different parts of the country. For an adequate understanding of communalism it is necessary to have in-depth studies of the problem at regional levels. In the remaining part of this chapter an attempt is made to provide some empirical evidence for the substantiation of the hypothesis formulated here.

III

What were the factors which accelerated the decline of the Muslim upper class? What prevented the surviving elements of this upper class from responding in a vigorous way to the new challenges and opportunities offered by British rule, especially in the economic sphere? In order to tackle these questions, it is necessary to understand not only the nature of the new economic challenges and opportunities but also the nature of the inherited attitudes and cultural traditions of the Muslim upper class, which created inhibitions and impediments in their progress. Both these factors slowed down not only the process of emergence of a new middle class among the Muslims; what is more important, they exposed them to exploitation and dominance by the new Hindu middle class.

One of the fundamental characteristics of the new economy following consolidation of British rule was the tremendous growth of the *tertiary* sector; what expanded rapidly was not the sphere of production but the sphere of *circulation*.[19] It is noteworthy that while non-commercial traditions or the lack of a business orientation and skills did not permit the Muslim upper class to benefit from this economic boom, their aristocratic pretensions or the attachment to the feudal prodigal style of life brought about their rapid decline in the material sphere. They were in fact pushed out from the leading positions which they had occupied in the largely non-commercial, traditional economy. In sharp contrast to the Muslims, certain Hindu castes and communities which possessed a business tradition as well as the necessary skills, thrived in the new economy; from them there arose the new classes of merchants, money-lenders and financiers, the commercial landlords who were the main products of a colonial economy. At a certain stage the new entrepreneurs of modern industry also emerged mainly from these communities. The new economy, therefore, was characterised by almost total 'Hindu' dominance.

A number of empirical studies have taken note of the economic decline of the Muslims in general, and the Muslim upper class in particular, on account of their attachment to a feudal mode of life. The following passage from the Report of the United Provinces Provincial Banking Enquiry Committee 1929-30 is valid for many regions of the country.[20]

> A Muhammedan witness writes:
>
> The main reason for the growing poverty of the Muslims in this province is their high cost of living as compared with that of other communities. The Muslim has not adjusted himself to changed circumstances and still adheres to the habits and ways which characterised him during the decadence of the Muslim rule in India. His standard of living is infinitely more expensive than that of the Hindu and always upto, if not beyond, his income. Hospitality, moreover, is to him almost a religious duty . . . . The charge of thriftlessness can be more justifiably laid at the door of the Muslim than of the Hindu peasant. His economic position is also seriously affected by the Muslim law of inheritance. In a Hindu joint family, widows get merely a life interest daughters get nothing, and the estate is managed by a *Karta* or agent. Among Muslims, on the other hand, the division of property after death is inevitable and often results in breaking up small estates into fragments which are not worth keeping. But though the heirs income is thus diminished, his expenses remain on the same scale as it was before the property was divided; for to cut down his expenses would bring disgrace to the family. The Muslim again is more litigious than the Hindu . . . Meantime, his family pride prevents him from taking up commercial occupations unless he happens to have been born into some trade, and even then he is rarely able to make both ends meet . . . . The natural result is that the Muslim fails quickly and easily into debt to an even greater extent than the Hindu. Yet whilst he is ready to pay the

most usurious rates of interest, his religion does not permit him to lend money on interest: and thus such capital as the Muslim possesses is often rendered inoperative.

The cumulative consequence of this whole way of life is the transfer of property from the Muslims to non-Muslim money-lenders. This is also revealed by the above Report in the following words:

> The general conclusion emerging from these figures is that whilst Rajput and Muhamedans have lost heavily, the consequent gains have not all gone to non-agriculturist classes. Indeed, by far the largest gainers are the Brahmans, whilst other agriculturists (which in these particular districts mean principally Kurmis, Ahirs, Ahars and Jats), have also made considerable acquisitions. And it can safely be asserted that of all these transfers by far the greater part was the direct results of indebtedness: and that the new landowners, whether Brahman, Kurmi, Jat or Vaish, are the moneylenders to whom that debt was due.[21]

The propensity of the Muslims to indebtedness has also attracted the attention of scholars engaged in studies of other regions of the country. Thus Malcolm Darling makes the following observation on the Muhammedans in the Punjab:

> There is one feature that must be noted in regard to debt in the Punjab. Though almost the whole amount has been advanced by Hindus or Sikha, neither being debarred by religion from the taking of interest, well over half has been incurred by Muhammedans. Forming 57% of the rural population, Muhammedans must few at least 78 crores, and seeing that they are generally more involved than their neighbours the amount probably exceeds 80 crores. No community can hope to thrive with so great a handicap, and if the Muhammedan community wishes to keep abreast of its rivals it would be wise to consider seriously how debt can be reduced and to support to the utmost any remedy that promises reduction.[22]

Darling also takes note of the Muhammedan's 'natural contempt for accounts': as a result, he 'rarely checks expenditure until his elbow is unpleasantly jogged by the moneylender'. Darling comments that this incompetence in money matters, combined with the prohibition against usury which he had inherited from the law of Moses, puts him at the mercy of the moneylender, who consequently thrives in the *Bet*.'[23] Moreover, in all parts of the province the agricultural money-lender has appeared as a force, 'except in the Muhammedan north and west, where they are still scarce.'[24] It is only in the Central Punjab that 'the Muhammedan agriculturist is beginning to square the precepts of religion with the claims of business had there are well over a thousand who have bowed the knee to Mammon.'[25]

Similarly, the Report of the Bengal Provincial Banking Enquiry Committee 1929-30 maintains that 'Muhammedans take only a very insignificant part in commerce, being represented by a few men from the Western Residency.'[26]

Apart from the landed gentry, the artisans constituted another important section of the Muslim community which suffered a serious set-back not only as a consequence of the decline of the feudal nobility but, more importantly, as a sequel to the development of the market economy. It should be noted that even though not all the traditional artisans were Muslims, the representation of Muslims in the artisan occupations was substantial. The artisan handicrafts sector exhibited two significant trends under the impact of new forces released by British rule. These are very succinctly summed up by D. R. Gadgil in his book *The Industrial Evolution of India in Recent Times, 1860-1939*. The first tendency, as Gadgil points out, was the rapid declined of some of the older forms of (artisan) activity, under the impact of changed political and economic conditions. The other tendency was the survival of some of the forms of artisan activity through adaptation of products, improvements in tools and technique, availability of new types or scarces of raw material and, finally, through total dependence on middlemen for supply, finance and marketing. This change in the organisation of artisan activity was more marked in the case of the weaving industry where the self-employed independent weaver had been replaced by new economic-organisational forms. To quote Gadgil:

> The predominant forms were, therefore, of a master-weaver giving employment to weavers, usually of his own caste, in their own homes or of a merchant of yarn or cloth or both doing the same, or a *karkhandar* bringing the weavers together in a small factory with suitable looms or other equipment provided for them. In each case the dependence of the weaver on the middle-man-employer was complete.[27]

The trend of growing subordination to, and exploitation by middlemen was not confined to the weaving industry alone; this was: this was the fate of all the artisan handicrafts which struggled for survival. To quote Gadgil again:

> Lack of finance and of contact with sources of raw materials or markets, when they were not local, characterised all artisan industry, urban and rural. The result was complete dependence on moneylenders and trader intermediaries, high costs and low earnings. The picture presented in this respect is the same whether in surveys like those of U.P. or Bengal districts in the early twenties or in the reports of the Bombay Economic and Industrial Survey Committee (1939-40) or in the official replies from various provinces and states to the questionnaire (1939-40) of the Rural and Cottage Industries Sub-Committee of the National Planning Committee.[28]

Gadgil sums up the general trend of change in relation to artisans during the end of the thirties as follows:

> The survey material relating to the end of the thirties emphasises not only the great dependence of the artisans on the middle-men but also the decline in many cottage and small-scale industries which took place in the thirties.[29]

It is safe to infer that these observations do give an insight into the fate of the Muslim artisans, since they constitute an important section of the artisans as a whole.

Lastly, the fact that in areas like Bengal, the Muslim peasantry was also exposed to exploitation by upper classes which were predominantly Hindu, is very sharply brought out in the following passage from Broomfields' *Elite Conflict in a Plural Society:*

> If history united the Bengali Muslim community, so too did its enmity towards the Hindu bhadralok. In search of an object of denunciation the communalists politician did not, like the nationalist, have to resort to the remote and relatively unfamiliar figures of the British Raj. He had an excellent target for attack in that dominant Hindu minority that supplied the landholders and their agents, the moneylenders, the lawyers, the tax collectors and other government officials with whom every Bengali Muslim, rural or urban, was forced to have dealings. To charge this group with tyranny and to call for united backing to break its power was a sure way to arouse popular enthusiam. And if anger ran to violence, it was the priviledged Hindu minority that was likely to be hurt most seriously.[30]

The great contrast between the Muslims and Hindus becomes glaringly manifest when one studies the economic decline of the Muslim upper class against the background of the rise of new classes among the Hindus. The new situation favoured certain Hindu castes and communities, who not only exploited it fully, but were so solidly entrenched in the new economy at all strategic points that all competition from late-comers was virtually ruled out. These developments are very well presented by D. R. Gadgil in the following passage:

> Another feature of the development of modern business is the concentration of trading and entrepreneurial activity in comparatively small sections of the total population. Because of the dominance of caste in Indian social life there has always been a high specialisation of occupational distribution. The trading and financial castes have been always highly urbanised and have rarely undertaken directly agricultural or handicrafts productive activity. However, it is these communities that had the resources and acquaintance with business technique required to venture in fields opened by modern business. A small number of these castes, therefore, chiefly supplied and continue to supply, in the main, those who occupy the field not only in trading and finance but also the entrepreneurial role in modern manufacturing activity. Caste and community bonds help to maintain and accumulate

strength gathered in particular fields and also the extension of activities to others. As pointed out above, the crucial economic position in relation to agriculturists and artisan industry is also occupied by members of these communities. Members of the industrial labour force and the technical personnel usually belong to entirely different sets of communities.[31]

That the trading, financial and manufacturing classes on the one hand, and the peasant, artisan and labouring classes on the other, belonged to different sets of castes and communities has also been stressed by Gadgil in the above passage. This peculiar feature of India's *economic* evolution during the British period was also responsible for some peculiar features of her *social* evolution. That the conflict over economic interests most often found expression through communal, caste or regional tensions was one such feature.

NOTES

1. To quote M. N. Srinivas: Historians have often claimed that a knowledge of the past is helpful in the understanding of the present if not in forecasting the future. It is not, however, realised that a thorough understanding of the present frequently sheds light on the past: *Caste in India And Other Essays* (Bombay, 1962).
2. Gopal Krishna, 'Religion In Politics', *The Economic And Social History Review*, vol. VIII, no. 4, Dec. 1971, p. 362.
3. Ibid., p. 375.
4. Notwithstanding the tremendous importance of the problem of communalism for the Indian subcontinent, it is surprising that there does not exist a single comprehensive study of this problem. One hopes that smaller studies will finally culminate in a major work on Hindu-Muslim relations, comparable to Myrdal's 'American Dilemma'. Recent studies on India like M. N. Srinivas *Social Change In Modern India* or Rajni Kothari's *Politics in India* do not deal directly with the communal problem.
5. It is my firm conviction that any work which makes a significant contribution to the understanding of the communal problem is also bound to make a contribution to the development of social thought and theory.
6. Marc Bloch, who made an outstanding contribution to the historian's craft, makes a useful observation on the analysis of the

cause-effect relationship. 'When it is a question of comparing two particular phenomena belonging to separate series. . . the delicate problem of cause and effect undoubtedly arises. On the other hand, to contrast two sets of dissimilar phenomena over period of several centuries, and then say: Here on this side are all the causes; there on that are all the effects, would be to construct the most pointless of dichotomies. A society, like a mind woven of perpetual interaction. For other researches differently oriented, the analysis of the economy or the mental climate are culminating points: for the historian, of the social structure they are a starting point. Feudal Society (Manchester, 1954), p. 59.

7. Gunnar Myrdal, *Economic Theory And Underdeveloped Regions* (Bombay, 1958), ch. II.
8. Ibid, p. 26.
9. Gopal Krishna, op. cit, p. 374.
10. How past history is utilised by classes and social strata is very beautifully described by Marx in the following passage from his *The Eighteenth Brumaire of Louis Bonaparte:* The tradition of all the dead generations weighs like a nightmare on the brain of the living. And just when they seem engaged in revolutionising themselves and things, in creating something that has not yet existed, precisely in such periods of revolutionary crisis they anxiously conjure up the spirits of the past to their service and borrow from them names, battle cries and costumes in order to present the new scene of world history in this 'time-honoured disguise and this borrowed language'.
11. J. Nehru, *The Discovery of India* (London, 1956), p. 354.
12. Ibid, p. 387.
13. R. P. Dutt, *India Today and Tomorrow* (Delhi, 1955), p. 227.
14. Ibid, p. 229.
15. A. R. Desai, *Social Background of Indian Nationalism* (Bombay, 1959) p. 152.
16. Ibid, p. 347.
17. What Marx said about India as a whole was in a sense more applicable to the Muslim community. In their case, 'the loss of the old without any gain of the new' was far more pronounced, imparting a peculiar kind of 'melancholy' to the misery of the Muslims, and later providing the basis for an aggressively communal consciousness.

18. Gunnar Myrdal, op. cit., Ch. II.

19. The importance of the sphere of circulation in a colonial economy has been noted by many economists. Paul Baran has drawn pointed attention to the prominence of 'merchants, moneylenders and intermediaries of all kinds' in underdeveloped economies. These classes are sustained by many factors: the development of a land market, the importance of credit for the rural economy, the role of trade in agricultural produce, the disorganised and isolated character of the markets in underdeveloped countries, etc. Baran observes: 'Real estate deals, exploitation of temporary and local shortages of various goods, speculation and arbitrage, brokerage fees for establishing contract between buyers and sellers—all yield sizeable gains to the skilful operators engaged in such transactions. The more or less chronic inflation in most underdeveloped countries which gives rise to black markets in foreign currencies, gold and other valuables, offers further opportunities for lucrative commerce, while the ever-present chance of procuring various concessions from government continually invites the resources, the energy, and the ingenuiy of the well-connected and affluent men of affairs. Paul A. Baran, *The Political Economic of Growth* (Delhi, 1955). p. 204.

See also:

(i) Gunnar Myrdal, *Asian Drama: An Inquiry into the Poverty of Nations,* vols I and II (London, 1968); (ii) Charles Pettelheim. *India Independent* (London, 1968); (iii) Daniel and Alice Thorneer, *Land and Labour in India* (Bombay, 1962).

20. *Report of the United Provinces Banking Enquiry Committee*, 1929-30, vol. I (Allahabad, 1930), p. 41.

21. Ibid., pp. 125-7.

22. Malcolm Darling, *The Punjab Peasant in Prosperity and Debt*. (Delhi 1977) p. 21.

23. Ibid., p. 63.

24. Ibid., p. 97.

25. Ibid., p. 198.

26. *Report of the Bengal Provincial Banking Enquiry Committee, 1929-30* vol. I. 1930, p. 30.

27. D. R. Gadgil, *The Industrial Evolution of India in Recent Times, 1860-1939* (London, 1971), p. 330.

28. Ibid., p. 334.
29. Ibid., p. 335.
30. J. H. Broomfield: *Elite Conflict In A Plural Society: Twentieth Century Bengal* (Bombay, 1968), p. 328.
31. D. R. Gadgil, Indian Economic Organisation, in Simon Kuznets, etc, (ed.), *Economic Growth: Brazil, India, Japan* (Duke, 1955), pp. 459-60.

CHAPTER 7

Romesh Chunder Dutt

I

Romesh Chunder Dutt was undoubtedly one of the great figures of his generation in India. In everything he did he seems to have struck a new path and achieved immediate success. He was one of the first Indians to get into the Indian Civil Service, and his career as a Civil Servant was uniformly successful. He held high administrative offices and, when he retired voluntarily after twenty-six years of service, he had already held acting charge as commissioner of a division.

He is reported to have held literary fame as his first love and he cultivated literary pursuits all his life. Throughout his period of active service a large variety of literary effort occupied the bulk of his spare time. One of his early publications was a history of Bengali literature in English and he also produced original literary works in Bengali. First came a series of historical novels, followed by fiction dealing with contemporary social life. He translated the Rig Veda in Bengali and did valuable organisational work as President of the Bengali literary academy. He next undertook the important and taxing work of writing in English a history of civilisation in ancient India. This required of the author a thorough knowledge of Sanskrit literature together with full acquaintance with results of Western scholarship. Dutt showed that he possessed both qualifications in an eminent degrees and his work was immediately recognised as a highly competent performance which made available to the general reader a full and interesting picture of ancient India based on the latest scientific researches.

His career as an official was marked by the great care and thought which he bestowed on all that he undertook. The results of this are in evidence in official and other writings. One of his earliest writings was a series of articles on the Bengal peasantry which were published in book form in 1874. His official reports on Bengal tenancy, when the Tenancy Bill of 1884 was under consideration, gave evidence of both wide knowledge and sympathy and were recognised as valuable contributions. And in the early nineties he elaborated in a pamphlet his views relating to village self-government and the village police in connection with the Chaukidari Act..

The driving force behind all his varied activity was 'service to the motherland'. Dutt recognised this as the cardinal idea running through the activities of the memorable literary figures of nineteenth century Bengal and it dominated his own life. His historical novels, his history of civilisation and his translation of the epics were motivated by the idea of acquainting Indians and foreigners with what was noblest in the heritage of India. His deep sympathy for the people of the country and his solicitude for their welfare are reflected in Bengal Peasantry and in the Economic History as well as in his political work in England after retirement.

It is clear that, among the reasons for his relatively early retirement from service, opportunity to take effective public part in political and economic discussions must have been the most important. The years succeeding retirement were more largely occupied with political work and economic writings than with literary pursuits. It was in the years after retirement that he presided over the Indian National Congress, conduct the land revenue settlement and famine controversy with Lord Curzon, wrote two volumes of the Economic History, did important political work on behalf of India in England, at one stage, in collaboration with Dadabhai Naoroji, W. C. Bonnerjea and others, and, at a later stage, in collaboration with Gokhale. It was after retirement that he served the Gaikwad and contributed greatly towards reforms and progress in the Baroda administration and also served as a member of the Royal Commission on Decentralisation. His was a very busy life, a life of varied activities, and greatly fruitful. Its keynote was profound seriousness of purpose; he combined acute intelligence with great industry, wide scholarship with a sense of reality, and wide sympathies and earnest feelings with tact and moderation.

II

Dutt retired from the Civil Service in 1896 after twenty-six years of service. It would have been possible for him to continue in service for many more years and his decision to retire was unexpected and unusual. It is generally agreed that there were two motives which led Dutt to take this step—his literary ambition and the desire to have greater independence for political work. He felt that he could achieve both these objectives by work in England, and settled in that country immediately after retirement. His biographer considers the main objects of his mission in England to have been the following:

"1. To form and organise an Indian Party of sympathetic Englishmen in England.

2. To influence the British Parliament through prominent members of the House of Commons.

3. To educate the British public in general, and democracy in particular, in Indian subjects, and to win their sympathy and support.

4. To appeal to the wider world of Europe through literature and history."[1]

He spent the greater part of the seven years from early 1897 to the middle of 1904, when he was invited to office in Baroda State, in England. In 1898 he was appointed lecturer in Indian history at the University College, London, and thus had a platform from which to lecture and an incentive to pursue scholarly historical studies. During 1898 and 1899, Dutt was chiefly engaged in his translations of the Mahabharata and the Ramayana, and in December 1899 he presided over the session of the Indian National Congress at Lucknow. In 1897 he had already presaged his future work by an article on famines in India appearing in the *Fortnightly Review* and by a historical sketch "England and India" published with the sub-title, "a record of the progress during hundred years 1785 to 1885." This short work contains many of the essential elements of the later Economic History and also, in part, sets, its pattern, though there is no writing on economic history directly in it. The work relates, in an interesting manner, British policy in India with developments in British internal politics. In tracing the development of British policy, Dutt emphasise Indian poverty and Indian famines, links them to inordinate British expenditure which impoverished people, and suggests, as the main remedy, that administration should be brought into touch with the people, should represent their wishes and feelings and enlist their co-operation and sympathy.

Early in 1900 Dutt wrote a series of open letters to Lord Curzon about land revenue settlements in various Indian provinces. These, together with other essays on famines and land assessments in India, were included in a publication which was bought out later in the same year. In December 1900 he associated himself with a number of retired Anglo-Indian administrators and submitted a joint memorial to the Secretary of State for India demanding reasonable restrictions on land assessments in India. To this weighty representation by ex-officials the Government of India had to make a reply and this was embodied in Lord Curzon's famous Resolution on Land Revenue Policy of India published in 1902. The Economic History was produced in the context of these events. All through his stay in England Dutt was engaged in delivering speeches and reading papers on Indian affairs and the subjects of these reflect his main interests and the trend of his thinking. The speeches and papers of 1901 and 1902 deal, for the most part, with subject like economic conditions in India, famines and the land question and with agriculture and manufactures.

In many of these, one sees preliminary versions of the finished material later incorporated into the Economic History.

The Economic History of India appeared in two successive bulky volumes. The preface to the first edition of the first volume, The Economic History of India Under Early British

Rule, was written in December 1901 and that of the first edition of the second volume, The Economic History of India in The Victorian Age, was written in December 1903. Prefaces to the second edition of both the works were written in August 1906. Dutt died in November 1909, and no later edition of the Economic History was issued during his lifetime. The prefaces to the second edition do not note any alterations other than minor corrections and some rearrangement of the material between the two volumes. The work has thus to be looked at as begin the result of labours during the years 1901 to 1903.

In order to understand Dutt's achievement and the impact of his Economic History, it is necessary to realise that it was the product of an administrator of large experience engaged in active political campaigning for obtaining acceptance of his views on economic policy and on political reform. Inevitably, therefore, the writing of the history was directed towards Dutt's views regarding the contemporary economic situation and the manner in which it had developed. Many of Dutt's contemporaries looked upon the history as part of the political campaign. The following extract from a short sketch of Dutt's life which appeared in print while he was still alive vividly brings out this point of view:

> "But if Lord Curzon had hoped to have the last word in this famous controversy, he had mistaken his opponent. Mr. Romesh Dutt had not been idle after the publication of his *Open Letters* and the submission of the Memorial. He had put forth all his energies on the task he had undertaken. He had collected a vast library of Indian Blue Books, dating from the commencement of British Rule in India, and consisting of over two hundred bound bulky volumes. He had ransacked these invaluable records, and studied the history of land settlements and industries, and the finances of India. And he prepared an exhaustive Economic History of India from the date of the Battle of Plassey to the dawn of the twentieth century. The great work appeared in two volumes, the first in 1902 and the second in 1904. It was the crowing work of Mr. Romesh Dutt's patience, industry and literary ability. It was a lucid history of the industries, trades and manufactures of India. It was the last word on

the history of land settlements. Lord Curzon's Land Resolution is scarcely read to-day except for official reference. Mr. Romesh Dutt's Economic History has already passed through two or three editions, and is studied by every Indian desirous of knowing the economic condition and history of the people of India."[2]

It is not to be counted as a demerit of any historical writing that it connects the past organically with the contemporary world. Indeed, it is now generally agreed that the main justification for constant rewriting of history is that the past or portions of it are thus reinterpreted in terms that are meaningful to succeeding generations. The intimate connection of Dutt's history with the contemporary situation makes it highly useful to understand how Dutt viewed this situation and how he conceived it had historically developed. An excellent presentation of his perspective in this regard can be obtained from prefaces to the various books. Some passages from these are pieced together below to produce a brief account.

The Indian economic situation at the end of the nineteenth century was dominated by famines. This is brought out vividly by the picture painted by Dutt in the opening paragraphs of his preface to England and India.

"The present year has been a year of rejoicing all over the British Empire in all parts of the globe, in India it has been the most disastrous year since the country passed under British rule. A severe plague has all but depopulated the great cities of one province; a destructive earthquake has ruined the towns and villages of another; and a famine. The most widespread in its area ever known in India, has desolated the country from one extremity to the other.

"But the famine of 1897 is only one of a series of such calamities which have visited India almost periodically within the present century. Famines are a thing of the past in Western Europe; in India every generation every period of twenty years, has its tale of distress to tell. The year of the accession of the Queen was marked by a severe famine which desolated Northern India, and counted its victims by the million. The year of the Indian Mutiny was the commencement of the next twenty years, marked by three great famines—the famines of the North-West, of Orissa, and of Bihar. The year in which the Queen assumed the title of the Empress of India was the year of a more terrible famine in Madras, which swept away five millions of the people of Southern India. And the year of the Queen's Diamond Jubilee has, unfortunately, been marked in India by another widespread famine which embraces the greater part of India within its sphere, and which in spite of relief operations, is likely to count its victims by the million. The years 1837, 1857, 1877 and 1897 are sad landmarks in the modern history of India—landmarks not of progress and prosperity, but of desolation and disasters."[3]

Dutt was greatly concerned with finding out the causes for the poverty and the lack of progress. In order to analyse the total situation he raises the following questions:

"Does agriculture flourish? Are industries and manufactures in a prosperous condition? Are the finances properly administered, so as to bring back to the people an adequate return for the taxes paid by them? Are the sources of national wealth widened by a government anxious for the material welfare of the people? These are questions which the average Englishmen asks himself when inquiring into the economic condition of any country in the world; these are questions which he will ask himself in order to ascertain the truth about India."[4]

The answers to the queries raised in this manner are given by Dutt elaborately in the two volumes of his history. They are also summarised in the prefaces to the two volumes, from which the following are brief extracts:

"The sources of a nation's wealth are Agriculture, Commerce and Manufactures, and sound Financial Administration. British rule has given India peace; but British Administration has not promoted or widened these sources of National Wealth in India.

"Of Commerce and Manufactures I need say little in this place. I have in another work (India Under Early British Rule, 1757-1837) traced the commercial policy of Great Britain towards India in the eighteenth and the earlier years of the nineteenth century. The policy was the same which Great Britain then pursued towards Ireland and her colonies. Endeavours were made, which were fatally successful, to repress Indian manufactures and to extend British manufactures. The import of Indian goods to Europe was repressed by prohibitive duties; the export of British goods to India was encouraged by almost nominal duties. The production of raw material in India for British industries, and the consumption of British manufactures in India, were the two-fold objects of the early commercial policy of England. . . . When Queen Victoria ascended the throne in 1837 . . . there was no relaxation in the policy pursued before. . . . . During a century and a half at the commercial policy of the British rulers of India has been determined not by the interests of Indian manufacturers but by those of British manufacturers."[5]

"Agriculture is now virtually the only remaining source of national wealth in India, and four-fifths of the Indian people depend on agriculture. But the Land Tax levied by the British Government is not only excessive but, what is worse, it is fluctuating and uncertain in many provinces . . . . In India, the State has fostered no new industries and revived no old industries for the people; on the other hand, it intervenes at each recurring land settlement to take what it considers its share out of the produce of the soil."[6]

"Taxation raised by a King, says the Indian poet, is like the moisture of the earth sucked up by the sun, to be returned to the earth as fertilising rain, but the moisture raised from the Indian soil now descends as fertilising rain largely on other lands, not on India."[7]

"Within the forty years of peace . . . . the Indian Debt has increased continuously, and now (1901) amounts to £200,000,000. The 'Home Charges' remitted annually out of the Indian revenue to Great Britain have increased to sixteen millions. The pay of European officers in India, virtually monopolising all the higher services, comes to ten millions. One-half of the nett revenues of India, which are now forty-four millions sterling, flows annually out of India. Verily the moisture of India blesses and fertilises other lands."[8]

"For one who has himself spent the best and happiest years of his life in the work of Indian administration, it is an ungracious and a painful task to dwell on the weak side of that administration, the financial and economic policy of the Indian Government. I have undertaken this duty because at the present moment the economic story of British India has to be told, and the deep-seated cause of the poverty of the Indian people has to be explained. Place any other country under the same condition, with crippled industries, with agriculture subject to a heavy and uncertain Land Tax, and with financial arrangements requiring one-half of its revenues to be annually remitted out of the country, and the most prosperous nation on earth will soon know the horrors of famine."[9]

We thus see a situation described, the queries relevant to its analysis formulated and the answers to these queries given so as to explain how the situation developed historically. Historical writing linked vitally in this manner to current problems can be made to yield solutions. For the problems of his time the remedial measures were indicated succinctly by Dutt in the following terms:

"The evils suggest their own remedies. The Excise Tax on Indian mill industry should be withdrawn; the Indian Government should boldly help Indian industries, for the good of the Indian people, as every civilised government on earth helps the industries of its own country. All taxes on the soil in addition to the land revenue should be repealed; and the land revenue should be moderated and regulated in its operation. The Public Debt, unjustly created in the first instance, is now an accomplished fact; but an Imperial Guarantee would reduce the rate of interest; and a Sinking Fund would gradually reduce its volume. Civil and Military charges, incurred in England, should be borne, or at least shared, by Great Britain, as she shares them in the case of her Colonies. Civil charges in India should be reduced by a larger employment of Indians; military charges in India should be repressed with a strong hand; and India should pay for an army needed for her own requirements. All further extension of railways from State-loans, or under guarantee of interest from the taxes, should be prohibited. Irrigation works should be extended, as far as possible, from the ordinary revenues. The annual Economic Drain from India should be steadily reduced; and in carrying out these fiscal reforms, representatives of the people of India,—of the taxpayers who are alone interested in Retrenchment in all countries,—should be called upon to take their share, and offer their assistance."[10]

III

Dutt's Economic History is a fully documented piece of work. Especially in relation to the earlier period, his main source was the large collection of parliamentary papers on the subject. Dutt has himself noted that one of the consequences of the transfer of Indian administration from the Company to the Crown was the cessation of the periodical enquiries on Indian administration conducted by Parliament each time the charter of the Company came up for renewal. These periodic enquiries, together with other information obtained by Parliament from time to time, constituted a wealth of data on which Dutt drew very freely. Long extracts from reports, minutes of evidence, etc., are a marked feature of Dutts's history. In relation to the extent to which Dutt quoted from reports, letters, minutes of evidence, etc., it is useful to remember that in writing his Economic History, Dutt appears to have had chiefly the English reader in mind. Therefore, he took great pains to base his case on the *ipsissima verba* of British administrators, officials and others.

Parliamentary papers, reports of specific committees and commissions and minutes of evidence tendered before them, the minutes of administrators and official correspondence form the bulk of the material cited by Dutt, especially in his first volume. However, it is evident that he used freely all available sources. He drew upon standard histories such as those of Mill, Kaye or Hunter, biographies such as those of Elphinstone or Cotton, Lawrence or Mill, accounts of tours such as of those of Buchanan, or of travels such as those of Bishop Heber, recollections and memoirs such as those of Munro and Sleeman. He quoted extensively from pamphlet literature, especially of the late eighteenth century and in relation to the more recent period, from settlement reports, administration reports, settlement codes and revenue manuals. The large bulk of the material used by Dutt was the result of official activities or enquiries and most of even the non-official material was on the level of special knowledge or expertise. Dutt's history thus consists for the larger part of statistical data and of narratives and accounts, evidence and opinions extracted from official reports and other sources and skilfully pieced together with comments and explanation to give a connected and clear picture of historical developments and of motives and policies directing them.

As a result of the type of material available to him and also because of the view that he held regarding historical developments, Dutt treated the British in general and, in particular, the British administration, whether that of the Company or of the Crown, as the active agents; the Indian people and the Indian situation are for the most part treated as passive. They appear as active only occasionally when they reacted in a definitive and, sometimes, violent manner when pressures went too far. Being centred on official action and policy, the economic history was linked with and usually preceded by an adequate narrative of political happenings. The political history was pictured as the history of reigns of successive Governors-General and Viceroys and their war of conquests, either internal or external. After setting out the political developments of each period, Dutt deals separately with a succession of economic subjects. In the economic history under early British rule, Dutt does not adopt uniform period divisions for dealing with all subjects and all regions. Here the narrative is more related to specific operations, administrations or events in particular regions such as wars or land settlements. All is then woven round the subject for which, at the particular points of time, there appear to be voluminous or important data. In the Victorian Age, on the other hand, he divides the total subject matter in three periods: Indian Under the Company, Under the Queen and Under the Empress.

The pride of place among the subjects dealt with by Dutt is given to land revenue settlement in both the volumes. The emphasis on land revenue settlement and the system of assessment and the pitch of revenue was natural. In India, land revenue had always been the main source of income and it continued to be so throughout the period covered by Dutt in his Economic History. The administrative structure of all governments was also intimately connected with this business of assessing land revenue and collecting it. Therefore, the land revenue system and its operation were of the utmost importance in shaping the administrative and revenue or financial history of the country. Moreover, agriculture remained by far the most important economic activity in India throughout this period, and the fortunes of agriculture and of the agriculturists were intimately connected with the pitch of the land revenue and the manner of its assessment and collection. For successive generations the difference between a beneficent and an oppressive rule in India had been that between a system of land revenue which was moderate and just and that which was oppressive and ruinous.

The British, unlike other foreign conquerors in the past, did away, to a large extent, with the systems and laws of their predecessors and attempted to build up an administration and land taxation system in the light of their own ideas. The British were new to the land and its peoples and, inevitably, the period of transition was painful and distressing. The historian had to deal with this transition in its three phases. The first phase related to the increasing intervention of the British for acquiring political possession. This led naturally to greater and greater unsettlement of the territories until the British finally took them over. The second was the phase of the take-over itself and in the earlier case, especially in Bengal, this meant a period when conditions were near to anarchy. Subsequently there was gradual restoration of order and the devising of the new revenue and administrative systems. The relative ignorance of the early administrators, their zeal, and the demands and needs of the Company—all led, even in the third phase, to attempts at collecting amounts of revenue which were in most cases ruinous to the peasantry. As these attempts were made at a time when the population had not yet recovered from times of war and anarchy, the consequences were apt to be severe and prolonged. Dutt found it convenient to organise consideration of all the three phases indicated above round the theme of the evolution of the systems of land revenue.

The system of land revenue and settlements continued to occupy the central place in the second volume of Dutt's history which dealt with the more stable conditions of India under the Crown. Dutt's thesis, as we have seen, was that Indian poverty was the result, to a large extent, of a highly defective system of land taxation. The defects which he pointed out were the very high pitch of assessments, their uncertainty and the possibility of periodic revisions taking up entirely any increase in the income from cultivation. Only the permanent zamindari settlement of Bengal was free from these. In the circumstances, Dutt's efforts were directed, to a considerable extent, towards tracing the various developments in land revenue theory and practice in the different provinces and relating these to the varying fortunes and levels of well-being of the cultivators there. The burden of land revenue in India was undoubtedly high, in most parts of India, during the first half of the nineteenth century: and it was high enough during the second half of the century also to be felt at every important relative change in costs and prices or in years of calamity. Land revenue systems were in flux for a large part of the century and principles of settlement and assessment were constantly under discussion. Dutt was able to make good use of all the material that the events and discussions threw up to drive home his points relating to moderation, long-term security and incentives to improvement.

In all this single-minded analysis and vigorous polemic, there is one feature in relation to which one feels somewhat doubtful. This is the description of conditions in rural Bengal and the emphasis on advantages of a permanent settlement. It appears hardly sound to attribute the difference between economic conditions of peasants in East Bengal and those in Peninsular India to differences in systems of land revenue. In his earlier work, The Bengal Peasantry, we do not find Dutt holding a rosy view of the condition of the peasantry in Bengal. The Bengal Peasantry is a remarkable work. Though mainly concerned with the condition of cultivators, it deals also with subjects like administration, village industry and taxation; and the extent to which these articles, written in 1873-74, anticipate what Dutt wrote after 1897 shows how Dutt had applied himself to a study of these problems at a very early stage and how he had reached maturity of judgment even then. The view he took in 1874 of the condition of the peasantry and the effects of permanent settlement in Bengal is well represented in the following quotation from the Preface to The Bengal Peasantry.

"It is, no doubt, a fact, apparent to everyone except such as choose to close their eyes at it, that in some estates, especially in petty zamindaries and unprofitable Patni holdings, Mathote is still freely collected to a fearful extent, making to our certain knowledge, the amount payable sometimes double of what is legally due as rent,—that in most zamindaries Mathote is still freely collected,—that in all zamindaries, probably much more than is legally due, is collected either by the zamindars themselves or by their agents as their special allowances on special occasions, —that zamindars still possess to an indefinite extent the power to oppress, harass and ruin their ryots in a variety of ways against which the law affords no redress, and that therefore in most places ryots are still held in as sort of moral servitude, and comply, without thinking of resistance, with the most unjust demands and orders of their masters. Such uncertain and even increasing exactions, and such moral servitude, make it simply impossible for ryots to save anything, or to learn to be prudent, provident, thinking beings, or better their condition; and we have therefore in the following pages advocated the introduction of permanent restraints on the zamindars' powers."

In view of the two widely varying views regarding the situation in Bengal, one has to hold that, in part, conditions in rural Bengal improved greatly in the last quarter of the nineteenth century and also that Dutt's later judgement was not absolute but only relative; when he wrote his history he was apparently thinking of the condition of the Bengal peasant only as compared with that of peasants in other parts of India.

The other important subjects with which Dutt dealt were manufactures, tariffs and foreign trade, railways, irrigation and public finance. In each of these aspects he brings out the effects of foreign rule and of British policy. From contemporary data, records and pamphlet literature, Dutt was able to document how the Indian handloom weaver was oppressed and how his prices were severely cut down through the operations of the Company, its British servants and their Indian agents. After the industrial revolution when the relative balance of advantage changed and English machine goods became cheaper, British policy was directed to pushing them by all means into Indian markets. As a result, indigenous manufactures declined and imports of foreign manufactures increased.

The contrast drawn between railways and irrigation works in Dutt's history and in the writings of a number of Indian publicists in the closing decades of the nineteenth century is also related to considerations relating to the base of the Indian economy. The British built railways, obviously, for two purposes. The first was strategic, for enabling quick movement of the military for guarding frontiers or for maintaining internal order. The second was "opening up the country". This meant, in British eyes, connecting distant parts of the country with ports in order to facilitate the sale of imported British manufactures and export of raw materials grown in the interior. Opening up the country did not, at this time for the British, mean initiating development of the economy of the country. As Dutt often pointed out, the old colonial policy still persisted. This policy regarded the colonies and possessions abroad as natural markets for the manufactures of the home country and as the natural source of supply of the raw material and specialised goods required by the economy of the home country. Dutt insisted that, whatever the apparent change brought about by the adoption of free trade principles, British policy was still the old colonial policy in another garb and he made effective use of a quotation from List in order to drive home the point.

In contrast with this role of the railways was the possible effect of a successful system of irrigation. Irrigation gave security to agriculturists and made agricultural production larger and more diverse. While both railways and irrigation demanded large investment of capital resources, the former exposed the economy to further and more intensive exploitation, and the latter provided, by contrast, the only means by which the base of the economy could be made wider and more secure. This reasoning was at the root of the opposition to heavy expenditure incurred on rapid expansion of railways and, especially, on spending moneys earmarked for famine insurance on railways instead of concentrating on the expansion of irrigation works.

Lastly, there was public finance to which there were many facets. The high level of land taxation was necessitated by the high costs of British Indian administration. These costs were increased by reason of expenditure undertaken on wars for the expansion of British dominion and for the maintenance in India of military establishments required for this purpose. Interest payments on unremunerative railways and other debts, home charges, remittances of funds to England by public servants and others—all these resulted in a considerable drain of resources from the country.

In this context the function of Dutt's historical writing was to make clear the sources of action, analyse the forces behind particular policies and demonstrate how successive developments were connected inevitably with foreign rule and the powerlessness of the native population and its leaders. His fully documented history reveals British manufacturers clamouring in one era for keeping Indian calicoes out of England and in another against even a five per cent excise on imports of English cloth into India; it relates how British trading and manufacturing interests concerned themselves with programmes of expansion of railways in India and how financial interests were able to secure for themselves state guarantees of interest in relation to the building of those railways; it establishes how often wars and schemes of expansion of political rule were undertaken needlessly and recklessly and how every one of these led to a greater and greater financial burden, capital and current, on India. As against the powerful political and economic interests who brought about the adoption of these policies there was only an occasional far-seeing British administrator, or non-official commentator, on the other side. The policies and the historical developments that followed them were thus shown to be the results of activities of groups holding political power. Narration of economic history of the past, distant and recent, led in this manner to an immediately important political moral, viz., the need for participation in responsibility by the Indian people.

IV

Dutt wrote at the end of an era. Soon after the publication of his history, a number of changes were initiated which transformed the situation completely within five decades. In the first decade of the twentieth century, there came about a considerable change in government policy regarding assessment and collection of land revenue, the construction of irrigation works, and the grant of popular representation; these changes were themselves, at least in part, the result of the efforts of Dutt and his associates. About the same time there began an upward rise in the prices of agricultural products, which had immediate favourable effects on the economic situation of a large number of agriculturists. During the First World War and after, all these trends were accentuated. Prices of agricultural products rose faster than before, and the Montford reforms set definitively in motion the process of gradual transfer of political power to Indian hands. In the economic sphere, the first revolutionary change was the acceptance of a policy of protective tariffs for specific economic activities after due enquiry. Also, with popular ministers in the provinces, industry, agriculture, forestry, etc., began to receive closer and more active governmental attention and assistance. Popular demand also arose, in most States, for reforms in the land revenue system. These made periodic revisions more difficult to undertake with the result that the burden of land revenue on the cultivator in most parts was less heavy even in the depression of the thirties than when Dutt wrote. After the Second World War and coming of independence, the transformation was completed, so that fifty years after Dutt wrote, the situation bore no resemblance to the one depicted by him, especially in relation to governmental activity and policy.

This historical development in no way minimises the importance of Dutt's writing or calls into question any essential element in his description or analysis. It happened to Malthus that the population situation analysed by him and which had characterised human history for long periods till the time of his writing changed rapidly within a few decades of the publication of the Principles. The basic formulation for the population problem made arrestingly by Malthus was not on that account rendered the less valuable or valid. Dutt ably presented the economic history of a century and a half and analysed its dominant trends. The end of the era which he described and commented on broadly coincided with the end of his life and activities. Therefore, his picture of the situation became dated. This does not detract, in any way, either from the merits of his performance or the soundness of his views. However, it indicates how the importance of Dutt's work is related essentially to the period of which he was writing and how his economic analysis is relevant, chiefly, to the characteristics of this important phase of the modern economic history of the world.

Dutts' was almost the first history of a colonial regime written from the point of view of the subject of a colonial empire. It contains, in essence, a preview of what came later to be called the economics of colonialism. It is interesting to see how ably Dutt anticipated a number of the features incorporated later in discussions of the economics of colonialism and, by implication, some features also connected with the economics of the growth of underdeveloped economies. Throughout Dutt's writings there is apparent a keen awareness of the connection between political thought and developments and economic policy. This connection was ordinarily ignored in contemporary economic writing in England. Dutt also carefully brought out what is now a commonplace but was then not much regarded, namely, the relation of economic policy to dominant economic interest. Having been confined largely to historical discussions, he did not, of course, get also to discussing, as Ranade had done, the relativity of economic thinking itself.

In relation to economic structure and development, Dutt's emphasis on the base of the economy is striking. He was obviously keenly aware of the need for a broad-based, multilateral and multistoreyed development of the economy. He thought of this development coming about largely by the 'surplus', left with producing classes, which fructified. In this emphasis, his thinking was heavily influenced by his environment. Excepting for the care and protection of industry and relief of agricultural distress, Dutt does not appear to pay much attention to the positive aspects of State policy and action. Indeed, his insistent complaints about high taxation and the level of government expenditure would indicate a preference for a lessening of government activity and outlay. However, it must be remembered that Dutt's objection to high taxation and expenditure is organically related to its leading to a drain of resources out of the country. In this context, Dutt and his contemporaries constantly contrasted British rule with that of even despotic indigenous rulers of the past. In those times, even the high taxation of a ruler did not leave resources to fructify in the hands of producers, at least the resources remained within the country and benefited some sections of the population through the outlay of princes and courts. There is thus nothing to indicate that Dutt would not have approved of the high expenditure level of a Welfare State.

In the course of his historical writings Dutt had not much occasion to analyse the process of economic development or to discuss the effects of foreign investments on the economy of a dependency as exhibited in the relation between England and India. However, the following passages from the `Conclusion' of his England and India reveal his awareness of the many aspects of the process and his anxiety to present a full and fair analysis of the total phenomenon:

"Railways and carrying steamers in India have been constructed with English capital, and the interest and profit come to England. Nevertheless, these improved means of communication benefit the country in a variety of ways, and not the least beneficent effect is the opening up of markets for surplus produce. Large tracts of the country, the produce of which had scarcely any market in the olden days beyond the local demand, have benefited by these new means of communication, and the prices of the produce have generally risen in India. But in this case also, the increased profit remains with the people where the State demand has been permanently limited. In the greater portion of India it is claimed by the State. Indeed, land revenue settlements are made for short periods in tracts where new lines of railway are under construction, in order that the benefits conferred by the new lines may be secured by the State at the expiration of such short periods. New products like tea are now grown in India; but they are grown mostly by English companies with English capital. The profit comes to England, and does not benefit the Indian agriculturist. And the special law under which labourers for tea-gardens are recruited has been described as 'slave-law' in India. . . . Imports of gold on private account, and not for purposes of coinage, have averaged annually more than £2,500,000. And it is fondly imagined that this gold is secretly hoarded by the cultivators of India! . . . . As a matter of fact, the annual import of gold represents the wear and tear in the gold jewellery, brocades, etc., which are almost the only luxury of the wealthier classes in India. The import of gold into India no more indicates the wealth of the Indian cultivator than the import of silk hats and kid gloves from Paris indicates the wealth of the British farm-labourer . . . . Trade and public works, carried on or constructed in a country with its own capital, are evidence of the material prosperity of the people. In the case of India they are profitable investments of English capital, and while they undoubtedly benefit India in a variety of ways, they have not secured the object of materially improving the condition of the agricultural and artisan classes of India."[11]

A remarkable feature of the writings of Dutt and his associates is their constant use of descriptive and statistical data. Their writings are full of concrete pictures of such phenomena as the level of living of the people. And they made full use of such data as were available in relation to national income. The skill and effect with which Dutt could use statistical data are fully exhibited in the concluding chapter of the second volume of his Economic History, and the following comment by him on the relation of the average burden of taxation in India to the level of the national income, has a surprisingly modern ring: "This is a crushing burden on a people which earns very little more than its food."

We are today well-placed to appreciate fully Dutt's concern about the lack of resources of the peasant and the effects of a steady annual drain on the Indian economy. In modern terms, a poor underdeveloped country with a low saving potential must continue to remain desperately poor if a significant part of its economic surplus is being constantly drained away. This is the central lesson and moral of the two volumes of Dutt's Economic History.

In conclusion, it is but fair to point out that Dutt was not alone in the views he formulated or in the efforts at their propagation. The role of the pioneer in this field was distinctly played by Dadabhai Naoroji, and a number of Dutt's contemporaries, Indian and English, elaborated particular themes or emphasised particular aspects. It fell to Dutt, however, to present a complete and connected account of the colonial phase of modern Indian history. And in performing this task he produced a massive work incorporating an enduring historical account which, apart from producing valuable immediate results, stands as a monument to Dutt's powerful intellect, profound scholarship and intense patriotism.

NOTES

1. J. N. Gupta: *Life and Work of Romesh Chunder Dutt* (1911), pp. 217-8.
2. Romesh Chunder Dutt: *A sketch of his life and carrier*, (Natesan and Co.) 1909, pp. 31-2.
3. Dutt: *England and India* (1897), Preface.
4. Dutt: *Economic History of India Under Early British Rule*, Preface.
5. *Economic History of India in the Victorian Age*, Preface.
6. *Economic History of India Under Early British Rule*, Preface.
7. *Ibid*.
8. *Ibid*.
9. *Ibid*.
10. *Economic History of India in the Victorian Age*, Preface.
11. Dutt: *England and India* (1897), pp. 130 to 132.

APPENDIX

Muslim Martyrs in Jallianwala Bagh, Amritsar 13 April 1919

Abdul Karim: born 1901 at Amritsar, Punjab, son of Pir Baksh, washerman, killed at the Jallianwala Bagh.

Abdul Karim: born 1902 at Amritsar, Punjab, son of Lal Mohammad, student, killled at the Jallianwala Bagh.

Abdul Khaliq: born 1859 at Amritsar, Punjab, son of Rahim Khan, worker in carpet factory, killed at the Jallianwala Bagh.

Abdul Majid: born at Peshawar, North-West Frontier Provinces (now in Pakistan), son of Rahim Baksh, killed at the Jallianwala Bagh.

Adullah: resident of Amritsar, Punjab, son of Pir Baksh, washerman, killed at the Jallianwala Bagh.

Abdullah: born 1899 at Amritsar, Punjab, son of Lal Mohammad, killed at the Jallianwala Bagh.

Ahmad Khan: born 1903 at Amritsar, Punjab, son of Karim Baksh, killed at the Jallianwala Bagh.

Ahmad Khan: born 1903 at Amritsar, Punjab, son of Dare Khan, killed at the Jallianwala Bagh.

Ahmad Ullah: born 1884 at Amritsar, Punjab, son of Karim Baksh, seriously wounded at the Jallianwala Bagh, died on 25 May 1919.

Ahmed Din: born 1886 at Gujranwala, Punjab (now in Pakistan), milk vendor, killed at the Jallianwala Bagh.

Allah Baksh: born 1864 at Lahore, Punjab (now in Pakistan) blacksmith, killed at the Jallianwala Bagh.

Allah Ditta: born 1874 at Amritsar, Punjab, son of Megha, killed at the Jallianwala Bagh.

Barkat: born 1899 at Amritsar, Punjab, son of Bhilla Sheikh, killed at the Jallianwala Bagh.

Barkat Ali: born 1881 at Amritsar, Punjab, son of Ilahi Bux, carpenter, killed at the Jallianwala Bagh.

Bheru alias Nizam Din: born 1901 in Hoshiarpur district, Punjab, son of Labhi Gujjar, labourer, killed at the Jallianwala Bagh.

Charagh Din : born 1901, district Lahore, Punjab (now in Pakistan), son of Mohammed Bux, labourer, killed at the Jallianwala Bagh.

Fateh Muhammad: born 1895 at Amritsar, Punjab, son of Ata Mohammad, dyer, killed at the Jallianwala Bagh.

Feroz Din: born 1900 at Amritsar, Punjab, son of Sher Mohammed, goldsmith, killed at the Jallianwala Bagh.

Ghulam Mohhammad: born in 1901 at Amritsar, Punjab, son of Rahim Baksh, washerman, killed at the Jallianwala Bagh.

Ghulam Mohuddin: born 1874, resident of Amritsar, Punjab, son of Mohammad Jan Butt Kashmiri, killed at the Jallianwala Bagh.

Ghulam Rasul: born in 1895 at Amritsar, Punjab, son of Ghani Shah Kashmiri, killed at the Jallianwala Bagh.

Ghulam Rasul: resident of Amritsar, Punjab, son of Samad Shah of Srinagar, Kashmir, killed at the Jallianwala Bagh.

Hamid: born in 1895, resident of Amritsar, Punjab, son of Ahmad Din Kashmiri, killed at the Jallianwala Bagh.

Hassan Mohammed: born in 1910 at Gujranwala, Punjab (now in Pakistan), son of Fazal Din Arain, student, killed at the Jallianwala Bagh.

Hassi: resident of Amritsar, Punjab, son of Sikandar, goldsmith, killed at the Jallianwala Bagh.

Ibrahim: born 1879, resident of Amritsar, Punjab, son of Imam Din, contractor, killed at the Jallianwala Bagh.

Illm Din: born 1899 at village Chak Mokand, district Amritsar, Punjab, private employee, killed at the Jallianwala Bagh.

Imam Din: born 1879, resident of Amritsar, Punjab, son of Murad Baksh, blacksmith, killed at the Jallianwala Bagh.

Ismail: born 1887, resident of Amritsar, Punjab, son of Miran Baksh, goldsmith, killed at the Jallianwala Bagh.

Ismail: born 1905 at Gujaranwala, Punjab (now in Pakistan), son of Nizam Din, killed at the Jallianwala Bagh.

Karim Baksh: born in 1879, resident of Amritsar, Punjab, watchman, killed at the Jallianwala Bagh.

Khair Din: born in 1879, resident of Amritsar, Punjab, son of Mangtu, oil merchant, killed at the Jallianwala Bagh.

Khuda Baksh: born in 1883, resident of Amritsar, Punjab, son of Wasan Saha Fakir, killed at the Jallianwala Bagh.

Mahbub Shah: born 1889, at Amritsar, Punjab, son of Mir Ahmed Shah Sayed, killed at the Jallianwala Bagh.

Mera Baksh: born in 1889, resident of Amritsar, Punjab, son of Nikka Kashmiri, potter, killed at the Jallianwala Bagh.

Mohammed Din: born in 1894, resident of Amritsar, Punjab, son of Karim Baksh, goldsmith, killed at the Jallianwala Bagh.

Mohammed Din: born in 1897, resident of Delhi, son of Khuda Baksh, took part in the public demonstration at Delhi against the Rowlatt Act on 30 March 1919, received bullet wound in firing by an army unit and died the same day.

Mohammed Ismail: born in 1912, at Amritsar, Punjab, son of Karam Din alias Kashmiri student, killed at Jallianwala Bagh.

Mohammed Ramzan: born 1895, resident of Amritsar, Punjab son of Rahim Bux Kashmiri, confectioner, killed at the Jallianwala Bagh.

Mohammed Shafi: born in 1894, resident of Amritsar, Punjab, son of Murad Buksh Sheikh, canal department employee, killed at the Jallianwala Bagh.

Mohammed Shafi: born 1889 at V. Dangerke, Zafarwal, district Sialkot, Punjab (now in Pakistan), son of Jan Mohmmed, shopkeeper, killed at the Jallianwala Bagh.

Mohammed Shafi: born 1901, at Amritsar, Punjab, son of Rahim Bux, killed at the Jallianwala Bagh.

Mohammed Sharif: born 1902 at Amritsar, Punjab, son of Abdul Rahim, died in firing by the police near the railway bridge, Amritsar, on 10 April 1919.

Mohammed Sharif: resident of Amritsar, Punjab, son of Mohammed Ramzan, mason, killed at the Jallianwala Bagh.

Mohammad Bux: born 1884, resident of Amritsar, Punjab, mason, killed at the Jallianwala Bagh.

Musa: born 1894, resident of Amritsar, Punjab, son of Jamal Din Kashmiri, killed at the Jallianwala Bagh.

Noor Mohammed: born 1894, resident of Amritsar, Punjab, son of Jhanda, oil merchant, killed at the Jallianwala Bagh.

Ramzan: born 1894, resident of Amritsar, Punjab, turner in a factory, killed at the Jallianwala Bagh.

Rehmat: born 1898 at Amritsar, Punjab, son of Nawab Din Sheikh, killed at the Jallianwala Bagh.

Rukan-Uddin: born 1901 at V. Thanda, district Amritsar, Punjab, son of Illahi Bux, farmer, killed at the Jallianwala Bagh.

Shamas Uddin: born 1895 at Amritsar, Punjab, son of Sikandar, goldsmith, killed at the Jallianwala Bagh.

Sharar Din: born 1900 at Amritsar, Punjab, son of Jamal Din, student, killed at the Jallianwala Bagh.

Shahjan: born at Peshawar, North-West Frontier Province (now in Pakistan), died in firing by the police at the railway bridge, Amritsar on 10 April 1919.

Sher Khan: born at Peshawar, North-West Frontier Province (now in Pakistan), died in firing by the police at the railway bridge, Amritsar on 10 April 1919.

Sherbaz: born at Peshawar, North-West Frontier Province (now in Pakistan), died in firing by the police at the railway bridge, Amritsar on 10 April 1919.

Taj Din, Hafiz, alias Mullan: born 1894 at Amritsar, Punjab, son of Ali Mohammed, tailor, killed at the Jallianwala Bagh.

Umar Behi: born 1864 at V. Dulla district, Amritsar, Punjab, Widow of Shri Iman Din, killed at the Jallianwala Bagh.

Umar Bux: born 1859 resident of Amritsar, Punjab, son of Ida Sheikh, killed at the Jallianwala Bagh.

Umar Din: born 1889 at Amritsar, Punjab, son of Mohammed Din, private employee, killed at the Jallianwala Bagh.